ENDORSEMENTS

"Brad and Drew have written an incredibly relevant book with the potential to influence a culture that is skeptical of evangelical Christian and LGBTQ reconciliation. They invite us into their conversation as father and son, evangelical and gay, and show us that love and dialogue are not only possible, but necessary and beautiful. The Harpers demonstrate what it looks like to come to the table with honesty and humility while acknowledging the fullness of who they are and what they believe. I want ALL of my friends, no matter who they are, to read this book."

—KEVIN PALAU
President of the Luis Palau Association
author of *Unlikely: Setting Aside our Differences
to Live Out the Gospel*

"Brad and Drew Harper are modeling what we desperately need in the world: having a compassionate and listening conversation about a subject that too often divides and polarizes. They have done so with bold craft, helpful and honest clarity, and an obvious, committed love for each other. Well done!"

—WM. PAUL YOUNG
bestselling author of *The Shack*

"Brad and Drew Harper's *Space at the Table* fills a cavernous void in the evangelical conversation around homosexuality. At once theologically orthodox and lovingly relational, this book will be enormously helpful to individuals and families caught in the painful space between evangelical belief and the real-life presence of a gay loved one. People should make a space at their table for these authors and their remarkably irenic book."

—Tom Krattenmaker
USA Today Board of Contributors
author of *The Evangelicals You Don't Know*

"This book is brave, vital, and future-altering. From the first page to the last, Drew and Brad Harper share the full complexity and compassion of their familial love. This book can save lives."

—Stephen Winter
award-winning director of *Chocolate Babies*
and *Jason and Shirley*

"In a world so often enslaved to political and religious ideologies, *Space at the Table* opens us up to the liberating power of honest and grace-filled relationships. Brad and Drew Harper welcome us into their conversations that humanize rather than demonize 'the other' in the complex discourse on sexuality in contemporary society. Whoever is committed to cultivating intimacy with their children, parents, friends, and neighbors in the present cultural milieu without sacrificing their convictions will find timely and enduring wisdom here."

—Paul Louis Metzger, PhD
author of *Evangelical Zen: A Christian's Spiritual Travels
with a Buddhist Friend*
Director of the Institute for the Theology of Culture:
New Wine, New Wineskins
Multnomah University and Biblical Seminary

"There's something sacred about being invited to someone else's table. It's all the rage right now. Tables, that is. Still, I've found that more often than not, we have a sense of community, not community itself. This book isn't a sense of community. It is community. Real tables are scary, threatening, and often dangerous. But they are at least real. *Space at the Table* is such a table. The table set before you is dangerous. But it's a table every follower of Jesus needs to recline at. This book will disrupt *everyone* who reads it. No one is safe."

—A.J. Swoboda, PhD
Pastor, professor, and author of *Messy: God Likes It That Way* and *A Glorious Dark: Finding Hope in the Tension Between Belief and Experience*

"*Space at the Table* is a powerful, engaging love story of how an evangelical father and gay son maintained their love relationship in the midst of enormous challenges due to such conflicting personal values. As I read the book, I wept, rejoiced, argued with the authors at times and felt the deep pain that Brad and Drew both experienced. The book also provides guidance for how all Christians might relate more effectively with neighbors, co-workers and friends who are members of the LBGT community.

It took enormous courage for Brad and Drew to tell their story with such detailed authenticity. Revisiting the pain and then writing the details so we could see and feel that pain with them had to have been extremely difficult. I know many families are experiencing this pain, too. My prayer is that this story will provide healing and hope for all the families walking similar journeys. Thanks Brad and Drew for telling your story for the sake of others."

—G. Craig Williford, PhD
President, Multnomah University

"When I read this book, I was reminded of this Jewish Proverb: 'When a father gives to his son, both laugh; when a son gives to his father, both cry.' Both Brad and Drew Harper have given each other the greatest gift a father and son can bestow on one another. Namely, the gift of unconditional love and understanding. For anyone who cares about putting the priorities of love and family in their right place, I highly recommend this book. Thank you, Brad and Drew, not only for this gift you have given one another, but for sharing it with the world."

—Jay Rosenzweig
CEO of Rosenzweig & Company

SPACE

CONVERSATIONS BETWEEN

AT

AN EVANGELICAL THEOLOGIAN

THE

AND HIS GAY SON

TABLE

BRAD & DREW HARPER

SPACE AT THE TABLE

Published by Zeal Books
537 SE Ash St., Suite 203
Portland, OR 97214 USA
www.zealbooks.com

All Scripture quotations, unless otherwise noted,
are taken from the Holy Bible,
New International Version®, NIV®.
Copyright ©1973, 2011 by Biblica, Inc.™
Used by permission of Zondervan.
All rights reserved worldwide. www.zondervan.com

This is a work of nonfiction. The events and experiences detailed herein
are all true and have been faithfully rendered as we have remembered them,
to the best of our abilities. Some names and identities have been changed in
order to protect the privacy of certain individuals involved.

LCCN 2015960380
ISBN 978-0-9970-6690-6
eISBN 978-0-9970-6691-3

Cover Design: Tim Green, Faceout Studio
Cover Image: Brenda Jacobson Photography
Author Photos: Brenda Jacobson Photography, Clarke Leland

Printed in the United States of America

First Edition 2016

16 17 18 19 20 21   BP   6 5 4 3 2 1

BRAD

First, to my beloved wife, Robin, who has been with Drew and me for this whole journey. Sometimes you walked beside us and listened and loved; other times you stood between us and called us back to sanity and fairness when we were taking verbal swings at each other. You bear the marks of those battles.

To Breegan, my wise and fiery redhead, who just calls a spade a spade. You always held your ground with Drew while secretly considering him your hero.

And to Corey, my radical X-Games daredevil, who has perhaps the softest heart of us all. You don't like to talk about difficult stuff very often, but when you do, you fill us all with wonder at your insights—usually in the words of one of your songs.

Thanks to you all.

DREW

For my mother, who taught me to love justice, and who insisted that I was a writer until, at last, I believed her.

To my sister and brother, who grip me tightly when I try to jump, and who lift me up with the inspiration of their beautiful lives.

And for Robert and Linda and Ryan, who will dance with me at the feast of the Bridegroom in this life and the next.

A NOTE FROM THE PUBLISHER

Dear reader—

Thanks for picking up *Space at the Table*. In doing so, you've become part of a very special book.

Part of what sets this book apart is the way it brings together an evangelical dad and an agnostic gay son for dialogue, humor, and honesty in the same place. That closeness makes for beauty. It can also make for some tension. Crafting any multiauthor book with skill and clarity is difficult, more difficult still when the authors are of frequently opposing viewpoints, and even more difficult *still* when those viewpoints are on a social issue as charged with emotion, pain, frustration, and identity issues as this one. Still, that's exactly what we've done.

To do this took Brad beyond his comfort zone, Drew beyond his, me beyond mine, time and time again. It also asks the same, with humor and gentleness, of you, our reader.

If you are a theologically conservative Christian reader, you will likely encounter sections of this book that will give you pause, and perhaps make you uncomfortable. Drew and Brad speak candidly about relational, sexual, and cultural situations that are often glossed over or actively avoided in "polite" Christian circles. That is one reason we believe it is so important to preserve those moments here, sometimes in detail that some might find off-putting—because glossing over things is not honest, and it's time for us to be honest.

If you are an LGBTQ reader, you too will likely encounter sections of this book that will give you pause, and perhaps make you uncomfortable. While we've done our very best to highlight Drew's voice openly and honestly, the fact remains that we are a Christian publisher. We've been intentional about setting aside biases and preconceptions, but this is still a book of tensions. It's also a book of love.

We've worked hard to make this a safe space for everyone—a space where love rules, a place where each of us can be stretched *and* welcomed just as we are. Wherever you come from, we are so glad you are here. We hope that the honesty and spirit of this special book impacts the way all of us live and love.

Don Jacobson *Publisher*

Ⓩ | ZEALbooks

TABLE OF CONTENTS

Chapter One

THE INVITATION

Join Us at the Table

BRAD

On February 10, 1989, I met Drew Stafford Harper. I loved him the moment I set eyes on him.

Since that day I have hugged him, changed his diapers, exposed him to the unique, and of course transcendent, cultural contribution of 60s and 70s rock music, watched him captivate audiences from the stage, and been deeply impacted by his profound observations of life. Drew is my beloved son. Drew is also gay.

This book is about our journey through a beautiful, happy meadow of father and son closeness which filled over time with mines of conflict over sexuality and morality, a conflict seemingly irresolvable because of its roots in my deep religious belief. This is the story of how our relationship survived that conflict, even flourished, though not without some scars to show for it.

I have been an evangelical Christian for as long as I can

remember. I went to a Christian college, a conservative seminary, served as a pastor for over a decade, and since 1999 have been a professional theologian at an evangelical university. I believe the Bible is the inspired Word of God and true in everything it actually affirms. I also believe that the moral principles of the Bible are meant by God to apply to humanity for all time (even though the way these principles are lived out may change over time and from culture to culture).

And there lies the conflict. I believe the Bible is clear regarding homosexuality: God intends for sexual activity to be between male and female married partners and does not approve of same-sex relations. The purpose of this book is not to lay out all the biblical arguments for or against traditional evangelical views on sexual behavior. But it is important to share my position right from the start because it is the foundation of the obstacles that Drew and I have had to overcome to maintain our relationship. It is the conflict that lies at the heart of this book.

This book is for those thinking through what it looks like to love their gay neighbor and who sense that love cannot begin with condemnation. Interestingly, my next-door neighbors are gay. But my first gay neighbor is my son. This book is about what it has looked like for me to love him—and be loved by him in return.

This is a book for evangelical Christians and others of conservative faith in relationship with persons who identify as gay. It is for kids who realize they are gay in a family where being gay is not okay. It is also for those in the gay community, especially those who have been hurt by the Christian community, who are open to dialogue, which can lead to better understanding and even friendship. This is a book for anyone—Christian, gay, or both—who longs to see true love bridge the difficult gaps between many people of faith and many in the LGBTQ community.

True love is possible only when we are honest about who we are. As Drew and I invite you to the table we have set in this book, we do not expect that you will sit down and just surrender your long-held moral, religious, or personal convictions or identities. You have the freedom to be who you are. As we find common ground, we expect everyone facing issues like ours to move toward each other not by going *around* their conflicting worldviews, but by going *through* them.

If you are the Christian parent of a gay kid, we invite you to consider what it would mean for you to walk alongside your son or daughter without sacrificing your biblical convictions. If you are a gay son or daughter of conservative religious parents, we invite you to believe that your parents don't have to agree with your sexual choices in order to love and support you. We may come to different conclusions, but if we are all humbly asking the hard and important questions, love can grow.

I hope that while reading my journey with Drew, you will resonate with our struggles and hard-won breakthroughs to the relationship we enjoy today. I hope you find what we have learned and experienced brings clarity, love, and healing in your own situation.

I hope what we've learned will help you engage your own relationships and our world more productively, and if you are a Christian, more biblically.

I hope this book will make you laugh. Some of the stories, especially those told by my coauthor, are hilarious. The two of us have laughed a lot during the writing of this book—welcome relief, because this is also a book about pain. In our collision of worldviews, collateral damage is not just abstract ideas, but *us*, bonded together through family and deep friendship, finding ourselves ripped apart by opposing views.

Finally, a word to the LGBTQ community. Can I apologize? I am sorry for how you have been treated by members of my own evangelical Christian community. You have been hated, reviled, persecuted, and lampooned. Indeed, since I was in high school the most common word I have heard from evangelicals about homosexuals is that they are "disgusting." That kind of treatment is an abomination, especially in light of the Bible's consistent message that God's fundamental attitude toward the world is one of love, and that *my* main responsibility in the world is to love Him and my neighbor. I recognize that as you read what I have written, you may find my beliefs and my approach to my son misguided, even dangerous. My hope is that the story of our relationship will illustrate that people who believe as I do have loving, deep, and productive relationships with persons of the LGBTQ community—that disagreement does not have to mean homophobia.

My kids would tell you that as they were growing up, the one thing I said to them more than anything else is that *life is about relationships*. If that is true, then it applies even to families, like ours, that have been torn by battles over sexuality. I am learning that the only way to stay in relationship is to come to the table, again and again.

I believe with all my heart that through relationship we can both retain our own views of the world and still come to a place of common ground, of love.

I believe that because I am beginning to live it with my son.

DREW

Recently, I was sitting on the airport tarmac in New York on the first leg of a journey to my favorite place: Cairo, Egypt. The capitol of the Arab Islamic world may seem an odd place for a post-evangelical, American white boy to feel at home, but some things in life we don't choose; they just are.

From the runway I saw a summer nor'easter building—no rain yet, but a black sky full of electric charge ominous enough to keep us grounded minute after agonizing minute. I checked the time on my phone over and over, knowing that if we didn't take off soon I'd miss my connection and end up stranded in Toronto. I had not turned off my "handheld device," nor did I have any intention of doing so; I've found through the years that takeoff is inevitably the moment in which I'll receive an important call from an ex-boyfriend, my probation officer, or in this case my mother, whose FaceTime arrived from my grandparents' open grave plot in the middle of Kansas. It was Nana and Papa's "going in" party, and Mama wanted me to hear the banjo hymns.

The burial of my father's mother and her husband had been put off for some time, because the ground in Kansas stays hard for a long while after the winter, something I learned as a kid when Nana and Papa's Labrador did us the discourtesy of dying at Christmas, obliging us to keep "Dory" in the deep freeze till June. Fortunately there was no trouble in securing a plot—Nana and Papa had selected theirs years ago. They showed us once, on a family vacation. Drove us to the cemetery, walked us straight up to the grassy spot and said, "See kids? Here's where we'll be! Right here, in the same town we were born in. Isn't that neat?! Who's hungry?"

While Kansas thawed, Nana had been safe in my aunt and uncle's closet, in a very nice urn. It was dark in there, and my uncle had tripped over her, but only once. There had, however, been some disagreement about travel arrangements on the way to the cemetery. "Nana cannot ride in the trunk!" My uncle cried, horrified at my mother who was ready to lower her in. "She was claustrophobic!"

So Nana rode in back, in the middle.

Just about everyone in the graveside gaggle had a musical talent, but since my uncle had forgotten to bring instruments, Nana's favorite hymns had been found in their banjo karaoke versions on someone's iPhone. That impromptu symphony was what flashed from my screen as I climbed toward 30,000 feet. Mom gave a cheery wave, turning the camera so I could see everyone passionately lining the Appalachian hymns that Southern white Christians sing best. *One bright morning, when this life is over Aaaaiiii'll fly awaaaay!* coursed through my headphones while I ducked low to avoid being seen by the airline attendants (especially the tan, solid one who I hoped would later ask me if I'd like to purchase any snacks). As quietly as I could, I took the tenor line.

Then the signal got patchy, then it was gone, and out the window I could see nothing of the city, only the flash of far-off lightning in obsidian clouds.

If the signal had lasted, I would have known all the verses. The songs they were singing, songs of humble walking with the Savior, of Christ's glory in this world and the next, of the Day of Redemption and Reconciliation that hurries toward us soon and very soon, are the songs I know by heart. They're part of the heritage that my Nana handed down to her children, including my father, and which he has handed down to me. You can disagree with your heritage, you can criticize the ideas it represents as truth, but you are *never* without it.

The songs of our fathers stay in us, through the sweet by-and-by, till the end.

Evangelical Christianity is my heritage. And yet, it's the rare Christian parent and gay child who have the kind of love for each other's company on a personal level, and fierce rejection of each other's worldview on a philosophical level, that my father and I share. If nothing else, a guy who teaches evangelical theology plus a guy who writes for a magazine called *GAYLETTER* make for entertaining dinner conversation.

Ours is a deeply personal issue that intersects one of the significant social crises of our day. According to best estimates from the National Alliance to End Homelessness, between 1.3 and 1.7 million youths go homeless at least one night of the year in America. Around 40 percent of those kids are LGBTQ.[1] The overwhelming reason for their homelessness is family rejection.

This is only the most visible fallout between conservative parents and gay kids. Less immediately noticeable than the queer kid sleeping on the sidewalk is the girl in an evangelical family who lives in terror that someone will discover that she and her best girlfriend from youth group have fallen in love; or the popular guy on the worship team who gets dropped off at the back entrance of the Christian counseling center every week to work on "healing" his orientation.

Then there is the other side of the coin, equally obscured. Somewhere in America this weekend is a mother singing in church with her hands lifted in worship like always, but behind her smile of holy peace she's inconsolable; her adult daughter has just come out to her. This mom knows what her beloved conservative church says about "the gays," and because she loves her daughter she's

---

1 http://williamsinstitute.law.ucla.edu/wp-content/uploads/Durso-Gates-LGBT-Homeless-Youth
   -Survey-July-2012.pdf

terrified that their relationship will never be the same. Mostly she just wishes there was someone who understood.

Our book was written for those kids and parents, for their extended families and communities. Our perspectives are biased—our experiences are those of the white, male, middle and upper class, full of the inadequacies that come with such privileged people trying to engage issues of social significance—but in this kind of a book we can only speak from what we know personally, and hope that some part of it is useful. This isn't a definitive textbook; it's an offering.

The important thing is that everyone comes ready to listen. Our table is set for the ones who thought nobody could see them, who have struggled to speak their experience because of crippling fear, anger, pain, and uncertainty. Here, at this table, I want us to have a conversation. No one needs to come away from this table changed in what they believe or how they identify for us to have been successful.

What my dad and I hope—and pray—is that we all come away more full of love and understanding for others than when we arrived. That we will find ways to keep the songs of our heritage alive while staying true to who we are. If that happens, we will have done what we were called to do; this table will have achieved its sacred purpose.

Chapter Two

CHILDHOOD

BRAD

I will never forget the night you were born.

You were our first baby, so the experience of witnessing your entrance into the world was overwhelming—nothing could have possibly prepared me for it. You were supposed to be born at home with no drugs, Mom and I styling ourselves as young, natural, noninterventionist types. You had other ideas. After about twenty hours of hard labor, broken water, and a slowing heartbeat, our midwife said it was time to head to the hospital, and *quickly*!

At this point in your young life you had no intention of coming out.

Mom ended up with lots of drugs and a Cesarean section. My first vision of your face brought to mind a startling moment from the movie *Alien*.

You were such an easy baby. You slept well, ate well, and wherever we took you, you just smiled and lay quietly in your car seat.

Then you turned one.

I think the transformation happened at the party for your first birthday. You were sitting quietly in your high chair and Mom put your cake in front of you. You looked at everyone, beamed, and buried your face in frosting. As you sat back up, family and friends roared. At that moment you discovered what an audience was, and you never looked back. From that day on, all the world became a stage for you, and all of humanity ticketholders.

As the years went by, music and theater became your way of life. When you were about seven, you began an annual summer tradition. Inviting neighborhood kids to our house for a week, you organized jobs for everyone to put together a Broadway musical revue, for which you served as director, choreographer, stage manager, and master of ceremonies.

You were also an early reader. You loved to imagine yourself transformed into the heroic, triumphant, tragic, and especially musical characters of the world's great literature. Reading stories together became a powerful bonding experience for us. As I read you books, it was almost as if you were transported into them. Soon you were devouring novel after novel on your own.

I remember one summer day when you were ten or eleven; as I was leaving for work, you told me you were bored, and asked me for a good book. I recommended *Tom Sawyer*. When I got home that same afternoon, you said, "Dad! *Tom Sawyer* was amazing! What should I read next?"

You developed a unique appreciation for visual art, delighting in visiting museums with your mother, and devouring the massive coffee-table books on art history in our living room. But more than just *viewing* art, you wanted to *create* it. One holiday season you presented us with a portrait of the Madonna receiving the Annunciation, which you had rendered in the cubist style and coloring of Picasso. We used it as our Christmas card.

By the time you were six or seven you had worked through the art of the ancient and medieval periods and had landed on the Renaissance as "your era." So while other boys were using cardboard for making indoor sleds to slide down their stairs, you were cutting and pasting, twisting and shaping your own versions of the sculptures of the Renaissance masters in our musty basement. With an X-acto knife and old Frigidaire  cartons, you created a life-size (for a seven-year-old) model of Michelangelo's "David." You imagined yourself as the master auteur, giving your energy to fill a small part of humanity's need for beauty.

You were still quite young when you discovered you were much happier doing the things girls typically did, rather than playing "boy's games," and you began to notice that you were often not accepted by other boys. You were never very interested in army men, frying bugs with a magnifying glass, or blowing things up. When the other young males of our sports-obsessed St. Louis neighborhood were beginning to swing bats and throw spirals, you were asking mom to take you to Jo-Ann Fabric so you could get material to make *The Little Mermaid* costumes. For your tenth birthday, a friend from church gave you a sewing machine, and you were as giddy as Ralphie in *A Christmas Story* when he finally gets his Red Ryder BB Gun.

What are boys supposed to be like, anyway? For your mom and me, the question became important, not as an abstract discussion in a psychology class, but in watching you develop from a very early age.

I will never forget your confusion and pain when you would come home from church or school and tell us of yet *another* birthday party where "all the boys were invited, except me." In retrospect, I don't think the issue was that the other boys had feelings of animosity toward you. They just didn't know what to do with you. They didn't understand your love for theater, fashion, and art. They didn't get your disinterest in sports.

And, at age ten, they were not reading *Great Books of the Western World*.

But soon confusion turned to ugliness. When you were in second grade, you came home one day and told me that boys on the playground were calling you a "faggot." I was so upset I don't think I even took the time to tell you what it meant. You would find out soon enough. It was so hard for you to grow into such rejection. That was also the year Mom found a page

in your school journal where you had written about a desire to kill yourself.

It is hard to describe how deeply distressing all this was to us. On the one hand we were amazed by your incredible gifts, but at the same time so troubled by how much pain and rejection you were already experiencing simply for being yourself. We were at a loss for how to help you.

Your mom and I, hoping to help a

bit, signed you up for T-ball. We thought it might give you entry into a world more common for boys. Just the other day I saw a picture of you in your uniform, holding a bat and staring at the ball, *completely* unimpressed. I suspect you were thinking something like, *If only this thing were a microphone stand.*

It's not that you didn't enjoy parts of it, but, as you once told me, instead of standing ready in the outfield and talking to your teammates, you were talking to their mothers on the sidelines, advising them on their next reupholstering project.

I contacted Focus on the Family and shared our concerns about your natural interests. The advice I got was what most Christian ministries would have given 20 years ago: "Tell him to do 'boy things.' When he starts to do 'girl things,' tell him, 'Son, boys don't do that.'"

"Are all conservative people homophobes?"

I wish gay folks would use this word less toward people who disagree with us on religious grounds. My parents and many of my favorite people disagree with my sexuality, but they are not homophobic.

But homophobia—the fear or hatred of same-sex love or same-sex loving people—is still very real, including in religious traditions and political systems. To me, homophobia is most useful in talking about things in the public sphere, not in private beliefs. As long as someone treats me with respect as a fully equal human being, doesn't attempt to deny me my rights as a member of society, and can be kind and comfortable around LGBTQ people, then they're not homophobic—at least in a way that I care about. —Drew

As Mom and I talked together about this "Christian" advice, we came to an important conclusion: whatever the results might be, to treat you that way would communicate one thing: "Drew, there is something wrong with you. You are messed up."

Instead, we decided to support you in the things you loved.

I don't regret that decision, and I would make it again. Now that you are a man, and a professional actor and singer, one of the greatest joys of my life is watching you perform, amazed at your gifts, thinking, *That's my boy!*

I'm so glad we did not discourage you from that.

DREW

So am I, Dad.

When I was six, we moved. You and Mom let me redecorate my new bedroom as I saw fit. By that age I had developed strong feelings about aesthetics and environment, including a conviction that the widespread enthusiasm for sponge paint in America throughout the late 1990s was a disgusting shame. The diseased pastel colors of my new bedroom were best described as "viral."

I replaced the chartreuse and pus pink with a sage green that was rich but unobtrusive, like a good uncle. I asked if I could have a wallpaper border, so Mom took me to the store to peruse samples. I was leafing, bored to tears, through cowboys and racecars and all the other "little boy options" when suddenly my heart stopped. *There it was.* The most magnificent border I could have imagined. It was as if the clouds had parted and God Himself had reached down and said, "This is the wallpaper I've planned *just for you*, my son!"

I begged. Mom resisted. Amused at my choice, she nonetheless appealed to practicality, wondering if I might not want to go with something *more* . . . with something *less* . . . something *not that*. I cajoled and groveled, ignoring the salesman who kept turning back and forth from this small boy to his chosen wallpaper with the kind of wide-eyed look people have toward the end of *A Clockwork Orange*.

Eventually, Mom gave in.

> **"Is my child's attraction to the same sex a choice?"**
>
> *Having talked to dozens of young gay Christian men over the years, every one of them has told me, "As soon as I realized I had sexual attractions, I realized I was attracted to men." Boys do not stand around waiting for the school bus one morning and ask themselves, "Okay, today I need to decide what I'm going to be—gay or straight, gay or straight . . . " Honestly, who would choose to be gay, knowing the kind of suffering and rejection they would face as a result? I am convinced that what a person decides to do with their attractions is a choice, but the attractions themselves are not.* —**Brad**

After weeks of waiting, the special-order selection arrived. You glued it to the wall, and I lay in my bed blissfully contented . . . surrounded by the buck-naked saints and prophets of Michelangelo's Sistine Chapel frescoes. Their gleaming, glorious bodies now paraded in a repeating pattern along the length of my new room. Mom suggested, as Pope Pius IV had done before her, that tasteful little loincloths be painted on, but I insisted that to deface the art would be *sacrilege*.

Once a kid came over and saw it. His name was Henry, and he was the first and only boy from second grade to come over to our house and "hang." Henry was fat, with ferret eyes and spiky hair.

Henry took one look at my bedroom and asked, "Why the hell do you have naked men all over your walls?"

The idea had not occurred to me. No one in our house had put it that way. But with Henry standing there glaring, *I* suddenly felt like the naked one, full of the newness of shame, like Adam and Eve after eating the apple. I stiffened, and shot back, "They're not *naked men*. They are *High Renaissance frescoes*." Henry eyed me briefly with patronizing compassion. He suggested we play outside.

"Is this my fault?"

This is the wrong question. Medical, psychological, sociological, and even theological circles are all over the map on the issue of what causes homosexuality. The evangelical world, especially in regards to gay males, has frequently argued that the most likely factor is a physically or emotionally absent father, resulting in the boy's sexual attraction toward men rather than women. But in many cases this issue is clearly not a factor. Trying to "fix" a gay person by addressing a false cause will do more harm than good. The best work I have seen recently done by an evangelical on the issue of causation is by Mark Yarhouse, a professor of psychology at Regent University. (See his book, Homosexuality and the Christian). *He argues that the best research shows there are many possible causes for homosexuality, finding out what it is in any particular case can be very problematic, and the most important issue is not finding the cause—which still may not lead to a "fix"—but helping answer the question, "Where do we go from here?" —* Brad

In terms of "cause," the issue at stake is that conservative parents, at least Christians, tend to see homosexuality as a kind of illness. When they ask the question of "why," does it

---

actually arise from genuine curiosity, or is it from a desire to "root out" the "cause" and "fix" their son or daughter into someone "normal"? The answer is probably a little of both, but from the child's perspective it feels like an attack. Cause is usually something that they can't even answer. The question puts them in a corner, and the experience is frustrating and hurtful. —**Drew**

Fortunately, you—Dad—would never have asked me to justify a room full of Michelangelo, and it was you that I lived to please and impress.

In my childhood memories, you are tall and broad like a Roman bronze, shoulders widened by your American cut suits—Brooks Brothers or Hart Schaffner Marx, and given to you secondhand by a wealthy friend on the church elder board. You stand behind your pulpit at the front of our church's cavernous sanctuary of red carpet, brown brick, and colored glass—the 90s middle-American mega-church to a T.

Your agile tenor still rises and falls melodically with a truth or a joke, vacillating between your two principal cadences: *BBC Radio Announcer* and *Incredulous Rabbi*. As a child, this distinction was important when I parodied you for your friends, along with your array of trademark hand gestures, including "French mime, resisting;" "souk merchant, haggling;" "Italian mother, forbidding;" and this one move where you'd stretch your arms out as far as they could go—your

Sunday mornings.

arm span growing vast like the California Condors you always looked for on our western road trips—and then bring them suddenly back together, pressing your palms like a yogi in Tree Pose.

I'll never forget those Sunday mornings. When you had finished your spell, said, "Let's pray," and bowed your head, I kept my eyes open to watch you, awed and adoring.

Balancing the force of your personality was Mom. My intimate moments with her were always about art. It was Mom who would take me to the St. Louis Museum to see Monet's water lilies, or to a traveling Broadway show, or to the symphony.

> **"Is this just a phase?"**
>
> *Maybe, but don't count on it. True, some adolescents who are basically heterosexual experiment with gay relationships for a while only to leave them later and go back to identifying as heterosexual. In my experience, for most gay persons—even those who, because of their religious convictions, decide to remain celibate or enter into a heterosexual marriage—same-sex attraction is a lifelong, enduring reality. —Brad*

Once, when I was six or seven, she took me to see Marie Osmond in *The Sound of Music*. I was dressed in a suit like yours, and on the way out of the theater, Mom held my hand as we crossed through the parking lot. I kept up a constant flow of conversation, peppering every few words with a loudly exclaimed, "Mom!" At one point, I stopped walking, turned to her, and asked if she'd like to know why I kept repeating "mom" so loudly. I leaned in to her and, in a conspiratorial whisper, said, "Well, it's because I don't want people to think that I'm your husband and I'm a dwarf."

I was not the type to be bothered that anyone would think I was a little person. What worried me was that Mom and I might be mistaken for a couple, a fear rooted—beyond obvious Freudian rumblings—in the reverent awe with which I viewed my parents' marriage. Twenty years later, the shadow of your picture-perfect union still hovers above me like Charlie Brown's raincloud.

You and Mom epitomized partnership. You were raised by a deeply religious mother and an agnostic scientist father, your best friends in high school mostly overachieving first generation Chinese, and the intellectual Jews of your San Jose enclave. Then there was Mom, daughter of an old-time evangelical preacher, yet captivated by the wider, "secular" culture, eager to unite her simple faith with sophisticated discourses for which she had much capacity but little exposure. The two of you completed each other perfectly. You were both—of course—virgins when you married. Pure as the driven snow. I remember you always honoring each other, never going to bed angry after a fight, and sitting together in the living room in the early mornings sipping coffee and praying for each other.

Praying for us kids.

Being gay, and far from a virgin (I'm not even a virgin with girls anymore), I realized long ago that I'll never experience what I idolized as a child: the storybook heterosexual Christian marriage. Strictly speaking, I wouldn't admit to wishing for it; but down where the heart lives, it's hard not to experience disappointment. It was a joy to grow up in the shelter of a perfect Christian marriage and family life. Once I realized I would never have it, I grieved. I did eventually relinquish the idea, but not without anger and sadness. I figure growing up is partly the process of deciding which of our dreams we will nourish and which ones we have to let go. What I won't ever let go of, however, are the little pieces, precious and contradictory, forming the ineffable paradox that is you: the evangelical Christian with eyes for heaven who somehow taught me to love this fragile, mortal world.

"How do you keep up with 'the letters'?"

Evangelicals will often ask us, "How am I supposed to address people these days? First it was homosexual, then gay and lesbian, then LGBT, then LGBTQ, now LGBTQI. How do I talk to someone without offending them when I am not familiar with the appropriate labels of their community?" Add to that the fact that the very thought of calling someone "queer" is almost unthinkable for most baby boomers because it was such a term of derision when we were young.

Our suggestion is that you simply ask people how they identify themselves and how they prefer that you would refer to them and then go with that. —**Brad and Drew**

From you I absorbed a love of history—whether watching you unfold the German Reformation to a Bavarian tour bus full of offensively-dressed Missouri churchgoers, or watching Ken Burns' *Civil War* so many times that our game to kill idle hours in the car was naming Potomac and Confederate officers until we couldn't think of any more.

From you came an absurdist sense of humor running toward the bleak, the British, and the Semitic: *Monty Python and the Holy Grail* (fast-forwarding through the part where the nuns try to get frisky with Arthur's knights), and your collection of Woody Allen's movies (plus his book *Side Effects*, which exploded my paradigms when I realized a person could make a joke about bringing marshmallows to a cremation), plus the Peter Sellers *Pink Panther* films,

and many classics of the Hebrew persuasion like *The Jazz Singer,*
The Chosen, and *What's Up, Doc?*

You nursed—like mid-century Hollywood's Sword-and-Sandal
epics—a Christian crush on all things Jewish. This would serve me
well years later as a New Yorker, but it was the rare seven-year-old
in Missouri who could recite the *Shema* in Hebrew. You insisted, for
reasons which remain obscure to everyone but yourself, that your
firstborn son be circumcised in a proper bris on the eighth day by a
rabbi, the sole anesthetic being Manischewitz wine squirted from an
eyedropper into my mouth. You read from the Torah and wore a yar-
mulke. In the home video, Mom's face says everything she's thinking.

Today, your taste for eclectic and exotic philosophical influ-
ences surprises my New York friends. They scratch their heads
when I assure them that the evangelical father who walked me
through years of ex-gay conversion therapy had also handed me
Jean Paul Sartre's existentialist masterpiece *No Exit* when I was ten.
How does that work?

This ramshackle mess of childhood memory unfolds to a
soundtrack of your beloved 70s music, heavy with The Eagles,
Fleetwood Mac, Clapton, Santana, Linda Ronstadt, Huey Lewis,
Neil Diamond, and (ta-daaa!) Barbra Streisand's "The Broadway
Album." Your fierce, almost religious aversion to "drum machines
and synthesizers of any kind" (code for anything recorded after
1984), meant that I never heard a single song by Michael Jackson,
Madonna, Cyndi Lauper, or Blondie until I left the house and moved
to New York City, discovering them in a burst of bright feeling.

Because I was usually lonely in those childhood years, I awaited
your late-night arrivals home with aching anticipation. I would sit
on our floor, poring through volume after volume of Will and Ariel
Durant's *History of Western Civilization,* lost in the black and white

photo plates, preparing to regale you with the things I'd learned that day. There was nothing as wonderful as finally being caught up in your arms when at last you walked through the door, squeezing your neck tight and inhaling the scent of your Ralph Lauren Polo Green cologne as you held me close. I doubt any boy has ever loved his father more, or had that love so unreservedly reciprocated.

BRAD

The intimate kinship we shared as father and son was so different from my own relationship with your grandfather. My dad and I loved each other, but we were not close.

My dad, as far as I was concerned, was a hero. When he graduated from high school in 1944, the Allied forces were storming the beaches of Normandy. He decided to do his part for freedom, and joined the Air Force in hopes of becoming a pilot. By the time his flight training was complete, the war was over.

In Korea, however, he flew fifty combat missions as part of a group called the Mosquito Squadron. His job was to look for enemy troops and then call aircraft to annihilate them, returning after the bombing run to survey the damage. He cruised barely 100 feet off the ground over the drop zone, his airplane turned on its side while he peered out of the cockpit. Only when I got older did it dawn on me that the last moments of each of my dad's missions brought him literally face-to-face with the broken and charred bodies of men who, just like him, had wives and children back home. I suspect that's why my dad never wanted to talk about those missions. But I was proud that my father was willing to risk his life for his country.

Another thing that drew me to my dad was that he was the

smartest person I knew. After leaving the Air Force, he spent the next four years at Stanford completing a degree in mechanical engineering. I think he liked being an engineer, but I also suspect he wanted to make his own dad proud, pressing forward into a space age version of his father's (and grandfather's) lifelong trade as a blacksmith. My grandpa had spent the war years building Liberty Ships at his forge and with his torch; my dad would spend his career designing spy planes and satellites to keep tabs on the Russians during the Cold War. In my young eyes, my brave, brilliant dad had risked his life to keep the world free, and now was putting his intelligence to work to keep the "Commies" from turning us into another satellite of the Soviet Union.

This was one side of the coin. The other was that my dad was an alcoholic.

The main effect of this on me was that, especially during my later childhood and adolescence, my father became so wrapped up in drinking that he largely withdrew from my life. When God gave me a son of my own, my commitment to be as present and loving as possible in your young life was in part a determination to give you what my own father could never give me, no matter how much I'd longed for it.

Finally, there was the issue that my dad was not a believer in Jesus. The brilliant engineer could never really place his faith in something he couldn't plot on his slide rule. This was our biggest disconnect. I believed in the Trinitarian God whom I could not see, and from whom I experienced love and total forgiveness of my sins. My dad, the rocket scientist, believed only in what he could see.

Dad spent his young adult years speeding through the skies, his middle years sending rockets into space, and his final project working on the Hubble Space Telescope, which would look further into the vast recesses of creation than anything humanity had yet invented, sending stunning photos back to earth of the wonders it saw. My dad saw the pictures, but he never saw God.

Like you, I was proud of my dad. I wanted him to be proud of me. This need for a father's approval, of course, would become a hurdle in our relationship when you moved into a lifestyle to which I could not give my unfettered approval.

Like my father and me, Drew, our relationship has always been deeply rooted in intellectual questions and conversations. Nevertheless, this life of the mind—a source of bonding for you and me since your earliest years—would later become the piece of the puzzle that led you away from the faith of your childhood, the faith I had raised you to know.

My life with my father shaped me as I became an adult, got married, and as I anticipated becoming a dad myself. Having grown up in a family where my parents' worldviews were at odds, I married a woman who shared my faith and my moral framework, a foundation upon which we built a life together. We hoped that our kids would come to share our belief in Christ and desire to live in a way that would honor Him. This, of course, in our minds included finding spouses of your own who shared your faith, and of course just happened to be of the opposite gender.

As I ponder all this, I am struck with the reality that

Brad, Drew, and Grandpa Harper, 1991.

there are thousands of other evangelical parents out there who, while the details of their lives may be nothing like mine, arrived at a similar place as married couples and as young parents, imagining, praying for, and counting on a future for their children much like Mom and I imagined for our own kids—a future consistent with an evangelical vision of God, faith, and the biblical family.

And then, like us, one of their kids turned out to be gay.

DREW

I also think of the kids reading this who see some aspect of their story in mine. They are heavy in my mind and heart as we've written this. Perhaps they always felt out of place, too.

It wasn't that I didn't ever have interaction with other boys. There were some guys at our Sunday school who weren't terrible, and there was our next-door neighbor Jack, a year younger than me, who is still a great friend today. Jack, however, was the terminally overscheduled son of a Catholic sports reporter, so between parish school, confirmation classes, soccer practice, and Little League, he wasn't around a lot.

So my principal image of childhood is definitely being alone and on the move, especially at school: shuffling sidelong through the playground, told to scram at every spot, like an Avon Lady in a Mary Kay neighborhood. I learned it was okay to talk with the middle-aged lady recess monitors, which is the relational equivalent of boiling oatmeal for breakfast every day—not thrilling, but enough to keep a person regular. I learned all about their lives: they were lonely, dissatisfied with their existence, and embittered toward men.

We understood each other perfectly.

The fact that I was a problem for the neat gender categories of Midwestern childhood showed up in things like the playground game "Monkeys and Raptors," which was the central part of every recess for first and second grade. All the kids played: boys were raptors, girls were monkeys. The point of the game was ephemeral—a lot of charge-and-retreat, secret strategy meetings beneath play-structures, and general tribal belonging. But one thing was always clear: I was never permitted to play on either team. The bluntly simple "Go away. You can't play on [the boys'/the girls'] team because you're not [a boy/a girl]" was something I heard every day, over and over again.

Eventually, I gave up asking.

I've heard gay men and transgender women talk about their experience as queer little boys who found their place among the girls when the other boys rejected them. This acceptance would happen for me years later, but for the first half of childhood the girls had no interest in making me their mascot, and I got used to a specific kind of crestfallen stomach feeling when the whistle blew to mark the end of another recess I had spent alone. Shouts of "Go away, faggot!" and "What *are* you even? You're not a girl *or* a boy!" and "If you don't get away from us, we're gonna beat your gay a** up!" stopped frightening me after a while. And then they stopped confusing me. And then I stopped hearing them, because I had learned how to be by myself.

An important step in fostering real relationship is rejecting the labels that we so easily give others. From the time we are kids on the playground, we categorize people, judging them by how they differ from us.

I will never forget Manuel, the first janitor I knew. He worked in the school I attended from kindergarten through fourth grade. He was short, old, and spoke with a heavy accent. I was too young to know that janitorial work was "menial." I just knew that at lunchtime, Manuel would come into the cafeteria to clean it, and that meant he would bring his cart! It carried his huge trash can, his mop, his bucket, and all his cleaning supplies. As the son of an engineer, I thought this compli-cated, efficient contraption was incredibly cool. But more important, Manuel was kind to me. In Manuel I found a joyful, wise soul who talked to me about family and gave me good advice about life.

Looking back, my friendship with Manuel was the earliest moment in my life when I began to be uncomfortable with label-ing (and often degrading) others on the basis of our differences. Now I believe with all my heart that to label others is always to degrade and diminish them as people God infinitely loves.

Parents, recognize that your son/daughter is more than simply a "gay person." Kids, recognize that your parents are more than the labels of their faith. We are all people, complex and beautiful. —Brad

What made the solitude bearable was that I never felt truly alone—there was always Jesus to talk to. I believed He was ever at my side, sharing in my fantasies of a different kind of future.

In developing a knack for walking around with my imagination to keep me company, or riding around on my bike for hours talking to myself and to God, I learned how to get high on prayer and solitary movement through space. It was a habit that stuck. Years later in New York City, I relished the ability to escape the insanity of my life by cruising down the smooth avenues for hours on my skateboard, day or night, alone with my thoughts.

And as unpleasant as it was, loneliness gave birth to the little joys of an overactive imagination. "Reftht," the country I fantasized into existence with my sister Breegan by the stagnant creek behind our local middle school, a magical country alive with complex royal decrees, aristocracies, constitutional law, and standing armies for the protection of its dual permanent inhabitants (Breegan and me), would never have come about in all its smelly, vaporous glory if I had been burdened with flesh-and-blood friends.

Childhood was characterized by silent expectation for some savior to whisk me off to the adventures I was surely *meant* to be having, someone like Peter Pan or Gandalf the Wizard or Auntie Mame, and those were the stories I loved the most. Salvation from the misery that was school, neighborhood, and playground could come at any moment. It was just around the corner! I believed it most deeply while wandering the Missouri woods, or standing on the hay hills of Nana's farm watching a Kansas storm blow in, or anywhere in the quiet desolation of nature where the mystery of life wasn't muted by the whirring of its mundane grind, or the tinny cackle of children who never ceased reminding me that I didn't belong with them.

"Why should I care about respecting my parents?"

When it comes to parent/child relations in America today, I see a vision of my inner crotchety old man sitting on his porch (he looks like a mash-up of Rodney Dangerfield and the Ice King from Adventure Time*), griping about how kids today "don't give nobody no respect!" Society too often accepts* *that an eye-rolling, hostile lump of flesh is how teenagers "just are." While that may work for some, I think that if you're gay, your parents are conservative Christians, and you still live at home, you ought to work harder than the average teenager toward building respectful, effective communication and gracious relationship with them. We all make mistakes along the way, but I believe that respecting our parents, even if we sharply disagree with them, is worth it.* —**Drew**

You and Mom vividly recall the note I wrote about wanting to kill myself, but I have no memory of it. I remember a fascination with death, and wondering whether Jesus would let me into heaven if I committed suicide. I used to wrap my hands or a scarf around my neck in the bathroom in front of the mirror and tighten it until my face turned blue and I fell over, and I'd memorized Hamlet's "To be, or not to be" soliloquy by the time I was in third grade; I liked knowing that I wasn't the only person who had considered the merits of taking an early exit. If I had grown up in the 80s, I probably would have dug punk, death metal, and grunge.

In writing this, I am aware of the presence, even now, of a disdainful sense of self-reproof: *Oh gee, you never got picked for recess games, boohoo. It's your own fault you never learned how to fit in.* During the years of adolescent ex-gay conversion therapy, under the assumption that rejection from other school boys had been the fatal flaw in my socialization that resulted in my 'perverted' sexuality, this disgusted recrimination became the core of my self-talk. I often thought, *If you had only been willing to learn the sports, the video games, the simple things it would have taken to conform, you wouldn't have been so miserable. What an idiot! You deserved all that rejection.*

I flogged that little boy Drew for a long, long time, and that didn't really change when I came out. Even after accepting my orientation, I remained insecure about my male gender presentation, pissed that I ended up as the kind of gay man who keeps a collection of fur coats and works in musical theater rather than the kind who wears Carhartt overalls and can change a flat tire in the parking lot outside the leather bar. Years after embracing my gay identity, I still berated you and Mom for not pushing me into things that I was sure would have made me a man's man instead of the sissy I felt I grew up to be. "Why didn't you make me do more sports? I should have been *forced* to play football, plain and simple. 'No Spring Musical without Fall Touchdowns!' This could have been a very reasonable axiom, people. You guys really fumbled that one up . . . (That's the right word, yes? *Fumbled*? Great)."

The long-held stereotypes about the "gender presentation" of gay persons—stereotypes like gay males walking with swaying hips and limp wrists, or lesbians keeping their hair short so it stays out of the way when they swing an axe—are neither accurate nor helpful. While these presentations may be true for some gay persons, they are also true for some heterosexual persons. Why does this matter? Because much of what we consider appropriate gender behavior or presentation is little more than a series of social constructs.

While the Bible has a lot to say about men and women, gender in the Bible and Christian teaching is not at all as cut-and-dried as many of us would like to think, and interpreting the Bible's words for today takes balance. Even from a more conservative biblical perspective, there is nothing, for example, that says men should not cook, clean house, or care about *their appearance, or that women should not love sports, carpentry, or bow hunting for big game. But seeing those presentations in a person and assuming something about their sexuality, or judging such behavior as inappropriate for their gender, can be very damaging. What makes it most damaging is when pastors and popular Christian writers present cultural constructs of masculinity and femininity as if they are eternal and universal gender standards given to us by God.*

On numerous occasions I have listened to young Christian men talk about a book all their guy friends are reading or a conference they have attended where they were told that real men are tree-cutting, chest-pounding macho dudes. Unfortunately, the guy sitting across from me has no such interests. He would rather be in the kitchen cooking or with friends knitting beanies for the homeless. He wonders if he is disappointing God by not being "more of a man." This kind of gender profiling in the name of God is unbiblical and destructive stuff. We need to put a stop to it. —Brad

Mom recently showed me that picture you mentioned, where I am up to bat at T-ball. The look I'm giving the ball is the same one I try to conceal nowadays when missionaries approach me in the subway: *Okay, I'll play along here, but I'm not having any of it.* That time I got in trouble for leaning on the fence, chatting with Mrs. So-and-so about her dining room remodel at the exact moment a fly ball appeared over the spot I was supposed to be covering, I remember the coach was upset not only because I had been kibitzing with this suburban housewife instead of manning my post, but—to add insult to injury—she wasn't even one of *our* suburban housewives; her child batted for the other team (something I'm sure Coach was concerned for in my case as well).

There's another picture Mom uncovered recently: I'm at kindergarten, wearing a scarlet sweat suit featuring Simba from *The Lion King* and a giant gold lamé turban with an encrusted jewel from one of my Aladdin-inspired "looks." The picture shows the other kindergartners staring at me in various shades of confusion, derision, or amusement as I pose in an "Egyptian Walk" (tiny misguided Orientalist I already was). My face is full of delight and pride.

A kid who felt comfortable wearing that outfit to public school in Missouri was loved and accepted enough at home to not care that the rest of the world didn't get it!

If you had listened to the advice you got from Focus on the Family, if you had discouraged those parts of me that boys "weren't supposed to do," the chances of survival for both our relationship and my life would have been very slim. The shame and hatred I would face in the coming years from a hostile world would be enough to nearly crush me, but the knowledge that I was *appreciated* by my family for the outlandish, "nontraditional" personality I was born with helped keep me safe from the deadly jaws of total depression and recklessness, even when things between you and me were at their worst.

Looking back, I'm so lucky. I had parents courageous enough to go with their gut, regardless of what their culture told them about what was "right" for boys like me.

There's a good chance it saved my life.

Chapter Three

COMING OUT, SORT OF

BRAD

From the day I entered seminary in 1982, I wanted to be a theology professor at a Christian university. Theology was a subject that had captivated me for years. Studying it brought me to a beautiful nexus: God reaching out to humanity on the one side, and humanity's stumbling attempts to understand this unfathomable God and the mysteries of His ways on the other. I wanted to invest my life in a community of people dedicated to this kind of study.

In 1986, your mom and I moved from Los Angeles to St. Louis so I could work on a PhD. In the process, we got "sidetracked." I ended up spending nearly thirteen years as a pastor. I had become content with the idea that leading a church, instead of in academia, was where God wanted me; but then in 1998 I received three separate offers out of the blue, each asking me to consider a position as a professor of theology. One of those schools was Multnomah University in Portland, near the

Columbia River between Oregon and Washington. Mom and I went to an interview.

We loved the school, the beauty of the Pacific Northwest, and the idea of raising you kids in a place where there were *mountains*, like in California where we'd both grown up. (The tallest mountain I saw in St. Louis was an overpass.) After a year of closing down our lives in the middle of the country, we headed west.

When we moved from Missouri to the Portland-area suburbs of Vancouver, Washington, you were ten and *so* excited about the adventures awaiting you in our new home. We enrolled you in a public school program for gifted kids.

Things seemed to be going pretty well until around December, when we were called in to talk to the school counselor.

He informed us that from day one you decided to tell your classmates that you were a Scottish prince who had come from the (fictional) island of "Haran" in the Hebrides Archipelago off the Northwest coast of Scotland. You used your best Sean Connery brogue to speak an entirely new language you had made up—"Haranian"—and kept up the charade. All day. Every day. Your backstory included palace intrigues, witness protection, and arranged child marriages. Owing to your powers as a storyteller, and since these were the last years of the age before Google, the subterfuge worked for about three months. But finally the kids found out you were jerking their chains.

Needless to say, despite your amazing ability to stay in character for such a long time, the deception was not appreciated by the class. They went from being fascinated with you to being disgusted, feeling tricked. The school counselor wondered why on earth you would do something like this.

How do you explain to someone you have never met that your ten-year-old boy has faced so much rejection for *just being himself* that the move to a new city gave him the opportunity to take on a new identity, one that he was sure other kids would find fascinating?

Now you found yourself even worse off than if you had just been yourself from the start. Not only was a little boy who couldn't compete with his male peers in recess games far less exciting than a Scottish prince, now the whole class considered you a pariah. Once again you found yourself on the margins, or, as you used to say to me when you were little, "outcluded."

I remember once that spring, as you were on the bus on the way home, the boys were talking about the birthday party they had been invited to that afternoon—the party of a boy who lived right around the corner from us. A boy we had welcomed into our home.

You were not invited.

Over time, the pain of so much rejection began catching up with you. You had always been a very dramatic kid, but over the first year or so of our life in Vancouver, you entered a pattern of emotional explosions that were troubling. I sought counsel from a professor at a local seminary who was a therapist, and he recommended a child psychologist. You began seeing her regularly.

DREW

"Due to what is probably a *crisis of masculinity* rooted in my lack of acceptance from my male peers, I am experiencing some *regressive issues* that are manifesting in same-sex attraction. How do we nip this in the bud?"

I practiced saying this over and over, muttering the carefully crafted phrase as I put the laundry in the dryer, putzed around the kitchen, stared out the front window past the giant cedar tree to our silent cul-de-sac, and then finally sat down on the couch with the phone in my trembling hand. Alone on a spring afternoon, a feigned illness having satisfied or exasperated Mom into letting me stay home from school, I was at last ready to make the call.

Arranged on the coffee table in front of me was a trio of pertinent sources: The NIV Bible, open to Leviticus 18; *The Collected Freud*, courtesy of your *Great Works of the Western World* collection; and *Bringing Up Boys* by Dr. James Dobson, scion of the American conservative powerhouse Focus on the Family. This trio of texts had been surreptitiously purloined from the shelves, their relevant passages quilted together to form my twelve-year-old self-diagnosis. Had I been jumping out of an airplane with a homemade parachute, I would have been less sick to my stomach. I asked Jesus to give me strength I didn't have, and dialed the number.

The dulcet voice of Dr. Adams, Christian child therapist, encouraged me to leave a message. Using my most professional, recently pubescent voice, I stammered something about an *emergency meeting* regarding *pressing issues* which required *immediate resolution*, and hung up.

The heavy silence was broken only by the ticking of the Austrian cuckoo clock, a souvenir from our recent trip to see the *Oberammergau Passion Play*.

The phone rang, and I grabbed at it like a junkie waiting on his dealer.

When Dr. Adams asked what was going on, I took a deep breath and pitched her my prepared diagnosis. I was sure that the subtlety of my analysis would help her see my request for her help as something like a sturdy corporation hiring a consultant, and less like Luke Skywalker being dangled over the sand creature in *The Empire Strikes Back*.

Dr. Adams's gentle sigh told me she wasn't taking the bait.

"Don't worry, Drew. We've been expecting this," she cooed, full of understanding.

Expecting this?!?!? What exactly does she intend by that remark?!? I sniffed, scandalized.

"Why don't you come in this week and we'll talk all about it?"

When I've told this story at parties, everyone agrees that it's an odd twelve-year-old who uses Mosaic Law, James Dobson, and Freud to come out to his therapist; what they differ on is whether or not a twelve-year-old with a therapist seems unusual. When the friends of my suburban middle-class upbringing had been supplanted by the posh Upper East Siders, boarding school brats, and Jewish American princesses of my late teens and early twenties, no one blinked at a sixth grader with a shrink. At home in the small-town Portland suburbs, however, this story generally elicits a "Why did you have a therapist when you were *twelve*?" Then I have to say something about "Haran," at which point, if he is in the room, my friend Zack Charney Cohen might pipe up, "I never believed him! I knew he was full of it," proud that his role as the only boy of Hebrew persuasion in our class had kept him Semitically skeptical.

> *People often ask me when I "came out," and I always tell them it's not that simple. There's this fantasy of "coming out" woven into American popular mythology: A kid sits their parents down in the living room, takes a deep breath, and says, "Mom. Dad. I'm gay."*

This typified "coming out" scenario constructs a template of normalcy by which a young person might feel like a human being while they spill their guts in front of the two people who they're biologically programmed to depend upon and socialized to seek affirmation from, knowing that they may, in certain cases, lose all of that in an instant, just for saying what they're about to say. This can embolden kids and calm parents, letting them both know that there's precedent for what they're feeling.

As nice as that universalism is, it doesn't reflect everyone's experience. It certainly wasn't mine, or that of a lot of gay people from religiously conservative homes. To talk about my "coming out" is to talk about a multilayered process that dragged on slowly over years, that in many ways is still happening—not because I'm private about being gay, but because I'm still in the process of finding out what that means. It's safe to say, though, that the process had its beginning in Dr. Adams's office the week of my terrified phone call. —**Drew**

Dr. Adams was big on "play therapy." Walking into a Toys "R" Us superstore is a similar experience to walking into Dr. Adams's office—walls of action figures, stuffed animals, dollhouses. Figurines spanning the full stylistic gamut from "Precious Moments" to "Hummel," all shelf-stacked to twice my twelve-year-old height. At the beginning of each session, I selected the toys to which I felt mystically drawn, and brought them to one of the colored sandboxes nestled around the room. I would arrange the toys in the sand, and Dr. Adams would ask me what the tableaux *meant for me.* I remember her scribbling furiously on her yellow legal notepads, reading the sand worlds like tea leaves in this mysterious voodoo ceremony of late-90s pediatric psychological ritual. All of this was scored to whatever aural flavor—rain, ocean waves, forest sounds, or embryonic *whooshing*—that I selected on Dr. Adams's sound machine.

For this big meeting with Dr. Adams, however, we were not upstairs in the playroom full of toys. Instead, you and Mom and I met downstairs in the conference room, where the walls were hung in pastel watercolors of beaches and gardens and other things that comfort grown-ups. I don't remember what I said to you, sitting on Dr. Adams's couch in that overly bright room. I remember the throw pillows—hunter green and burgundy and dull grey—and that I held them very tightly to my chest, and in front of my crotch. I remember that my face burned so hot with shame, and that you told me very firmly to look you in the eye so you could tell me you loved me and were not mad at me or ashamed of me. I refused to look at you until you insisted sharply, and even then I seem to remember peering out from under the sheltering dark of my hand pressed against my brow.

> **"How do I deal with the shock?"**
>
> *As a religious parent, you are generally going to find yourself in one of two places when your kid comes out to you. Either you have already seen some things that have caused you to wonder, or your child's revelation totally blindsides you. Regardless, you will experience some measure of shock.*
>
> *For some parents, it might be like one of those scenes in a war movie where a grenade explodes far enough away from a soldier not to kill him, but close enough that for several minutes he cannot hear or speak. If this is you, it's probably best not to do much of either right away.*

Honesty, love, and simple transparency are the best responses. You might simply say to your child, "Thanks for telling me this. I'm sure it was very difficult for you and took a lot of courage. I want to talk to you about this, but I am going to need some time to gather my thoughts and feelings before I do. Is that okay?" At which point it is very possible that your child will be relieved, since just the experience of telling you their secret may have been like leaping off the Golden Gate Bridge with a bungee cord labeled "Army Surplus—For full effectiveness use before 1975." A few hours, or even a day, to think and pray might be helpful for both of you before moving forward.

You may feel the need for strong, immediate action. Don't do it. This is one of the most important pieces of advice I can give you, and I wish someone had said this to me before I started to react. —**Brad**

It was at this moment that Mom did something I will never forget. She told me, there with you and another adult right next to her, how once when she was a little girl she had been excited by pictures of naked women she accidentally saw in a *Playboy* magazine.

How compassionate, how selfless, how *just* like Mom to reach down into my filthy pain and unbearable shame by exposing herself, pulling out a long-ago moment of transgressive vulnerability to meet me in the pig's trough and sit down with me in the slop. It wasn't very "evangelical"—with all our codes of moral righteousness—but it sure felt *Christlike*.

Suddenly I was a human being again, because someone had grabbed me and embraced me, leprosy and all.

From the mother . . .

From the earliest time I can remember, I wanted to be a mother. When I played house in the church nursery, I always had to be the mom, and I was very bossy, so I usually got my way. So when my firstborn came into the world, I was filled with an indescribable joy. On the occasion, my best friend wrote to me in a card, which I still have, "I hereby bestow upon you the New Mother's Medal of Honor and the Purple Heart . . . for bravery." In addition she gave me " . . . the Can-You-Top-That? Award for having one of the best labor-and-delivery horror stories of '89." Little did we know then that drama would continue to be Drew's life. From day one, like the process of his birth, being Drew's mom has been not only one of the hardest things I have ever done in my life, but has also been the source of some of the most incredible joy.

Several years ago, Brad and I were with another couple after church. I commented how much I loved their Christmas card. It was a candid backyard photo of their family, laughing and holding their beautiful, unmarried, obviously pregnant daughter sideways, all of them about to fall over. I said how great it was that in spite of her unplanned pregnancy, she was front and center. Her mom immediately replied, "Well, we're not ashamed of our daughter." While not intended, it was a loud-and-clear rebuke.

I had to ask myself if that was what I communicated about my openly gay son—"we're not ashamed." I couldn't answer yes then. But I can now. And I say

Mother and son tea party, 1993.

it as often as I can, especially to families who are blindsided by their sons and daughters coming out and shamed by their church communities. I am not ashamed of my beautiful son.

When families are walking this road, it's tempting to just focus on sexuality because it is a huge part of the story. But Drew is not one-dimensional. He is not just a gay man. He is a warm, funny, sensitive, articulate, kind, talented, courageous human being. He is one of my favorite people in the world.

Last Christmas, Drew played Ebenezer Scrooge in our local production of A Christmas Carol. I teach young students in an alternative learning environment, so a colleague and I made plans to present a Readers' Theater version of the play with our classes, inviting Drew to come in and read the part of Scrooge. I was thrilled when he agreed to do it. Never one to do anything halfheartedly, Drew arrived on campus in full-costume—Victorian era nightshirt and tasseled cap— and fully in character. He knocked on the window of what he thought was my room—where he had been the previous year. Unbeknownst to him, I had moved classrooms, and another colleague was trying to conduct class. When she saw this odd character in his "pajamas," she was alarmed. Despite his continual knocking with his wooden cane and trying to explain—in the grating rasp of an irritated Scrooge—that he was supposed to be there, she wouldn't let him in, and was getting ready to call for a lockdown. I'm not sure what happened next, but eventually Drew got to the right room and gave a fantastic performance, including a Q & A afterwards. I observed as Drew graciously interacted with the kids. One boy was a budding actor who was taking a drama class and loving it. Drew encouraged him to work hard and follow his heart. I was so proud to be Drew's mom that day. I didn't know what had happened earlier until a friend told me many *months later. As I reflected on this story, it hit me that it is a metaphor of his life: wholehearted expression, being misunderstood, feared, rejected, but having so much to give—if allowed in.*

The last few lines of my dear friend's note when Drew was born were prophetic: " . . . If you're like I was, you will fall in love with him one of these days. Little boys are such heart-stealers."

I have. And he is. —Robin Harper

I don't remember how the subject of the Stumptown Fellowship, our local chapter of "ex-gay" ministry Exodus International, got brought up. I've never had cancer, but being told as a twelve-year-old that there was a place for "people like me" to find a way out of our quagmire was the closest I've experienced to being told that "there's an experimental new treatment that's been working well in trials," and maybe, just *maybe*, could offer me hope for my terminal diagnosis.

Perhaps readers who didn't grow up in the conservative American Christian subculture will consider a cancer comparison inappropriate, but I mean what I say. To be homosexual in the American evangelical church, especially fifteen years ago, is to be *dead*. You are no longer part of the entity that has grown and nurtured and known you. You are cut off, disinherited from the promises of this life and the next that form the core of our ideological framework. You are an outcast, an orphan, a refugee. A diseased person.

To be a naturally-born *heterosexual* afflicted with and working hard to beat the "human ailment" of homosexuality, however, now *that* is a way to avoid the death sentence. What exhausting fear an evangelical child experiences in disclosing these feelings to her parents, and what sweet relief she finds in the reprieve that ex-gay therapy promises. I certainly felt it.

Leaving Dr. Adams's office, I walked into the cool night air with hope for a cure. *Thank God*, I thought then, *that I have parents who love me enough to find a place like Stumptown Fellowship for me to go.*

BRAD

After years of wondering about your sexual attractions, the question for your mom and me was, "What do we do now?" When you came out to us, your emotions clearly said, "I need some help with this, Mom and Dad." In light of that, we felt it was important for us to enter in. We wanted you to know immediately that we loved you unconditionally for who *you* were, and that we would walk with you on this journey. But we also had to respond to all this on the basis of our foundational commitments and beliefs about God.

"What should I do first?"

Listen! The biblical Book of James states that wise people should be "quick to hear, slow to speak, and slow to anger." That advice is joined by other passages, such as, "To answer before listening—that is folly and shame" (Proverbs 18:13). There is no better basic theme for evangelical parents when their child comes out to them as gay. Listen! One of the crucial reasons is that this revelation is not fundamentally about you; it's about them.

Your deepest concerns should not be about your shame, your future plans, or your reputation. It should be about the wellbeing of your child. This is not just your child rebelling, or "doing this to you." Approaching it that way will subvert possibility for positive relationship with your gay child in the future. With that being said, even if your initial reactions are about concern for your kid, as a Christian this will likely still mean heartache for you. Maybe even anger. Honesty with that is okay. Just make sure your emotions are rooted in love for them rather than concern for yourself.

This begins with listening first, and listening a lot. —**Brad**

As evangelical Christians, your Mom and I had been brought up to believe that the Bible is the inspired Word of God and its moral judgments must be taken seriously. Both of us also believed it was through the Bible and the Church that we had personally encountered the risen Christ. These are commitments that your Mom and I still hold to, not because we want to or because we feel like we need some kind of belief system in order to survive, but because we have been captivated by the love of God for us in his Son Jesus. Later at this table we can dialogue more about the Bible and its issues around sexuality, but for now I will simply say that we believed the Bible to be very clear that gay sex is not okay with God. We also believed that God called us to teach you about Him and what it looks like to follow Him. At this point in your life, you also were drawn to the story of Jesus and wanted to follow His ways.

So at that point, two things happened—one that I will always treasure, and the other which became a problem over

45

time. The first was that you and I began to take long walks in the neighborhood at night, usually with Chip (our Chocolate Labrador Retriever) as a companion. Sometimes I smoked a pipe, and I even gave you one of my old ones when you were a teenager. Perhaps it was just one small way of allowing you to do something adult, given that the rejection and confusion you were coping with was something no child should have to endure.

"I accidentally found out my child is gay. What do I do?"

This wasn't our experience, but it is important to consider. Parents, both Christian and otherwise, have differing opinions on how invasive parents have a right to be in order to find out what their kids are doing in life that they might disapprove of. Is it okay to secretly look through your kids' text messages to find out who they are talking to and what they are doing? Is it okay to look through their bedroom drawers while they are gone? I'm not going to take on that issue here. My own inclinations are that if you have real concerns that your child is involved in something that is a threat to their basic safety, then yes, definitely, this kind of search and seizure is legitimate. In most other cases, probably not.

But sometimes we parents discover troubling issues in our kids' lives simply through the process of vacuuming or putting away underwear. And in these cases, my advice is to be honest with your child. Tell them that you stumbled across something that worried you in the normal process of daily life, that you weren't ransacking their room. Then tell them that you are concerned and ask them if they are willing to talk about it. Even if they don't want to talk about it at that point, they now know the cat is out of the bag and will probably be willing to talk later. You just might need to be patient. Remember, in this situation you brought it up, not them, and they simply may not be ready. —Brad

The other thing was that I began taking you to regular counseling with a leader from a local ex-gay ministry. I have to say that I do not really know exactly what went on in your counseling meetings. I felt it was important to let the process stay between you and the counselor. You did indicate at the time that it was enjoyable and helpful to you. It would be years before I came to understand the damage it had done to you.

What I do know about was the conversations we had on our walks. Those were precious times for me. It was during those few years that I was not just watching your painful circumstances, as I had when you were a little boy; now you were growing in your ability to express your experiences in more complex ways. We talked a lot about how God could be present in the midst of your pain and struggles. Perhaps surprisingly, the most common struggle you talked about was not your sexual attractions, but your desire to have male buddies, guys who accepted you into their community, who you could just hang out with. Guys who would invite you over to watch a movie or play video games. (Even though at the very word you would morph into Glenn Close's Cruella De Vil from *101 Dalmatians*, exclaiming "Video Games!?!? Those horrid noisy things that children play with all day long, somebody actually designs them?! What a wasteful thing to do with your life!" You nonetheless still longed for the invitation.)

> **"What should I say first?"**
> *Affirm your love and personal acceptance for your kid—no matter what. Chances are your child knows you will not be overjoyed by their revelation. They may worry about how you will respond.*

Part of my daily life is talking to God about things about me that I'm pretty sure don't make Him happy. I can do this because I know that my heavenly Father's response to me is always rooted in unwavering love. While He may want me to grow, He embraces me just as I am. As parents, God calls us to respond to our children in the same way.

Your gay child needs to know from the very beginning that your love for them will never change, even if they choose to live their lives in a way you disagree with. Only this response makes it possible to move forward in loving relationship.

"What questions should I ask?"

Ask your child to tell you what has led them to the conclusion that they're gay. This does a couple of important things. First, it communicates to your child that you are going to try to understand where they are coming from. Second, it will give you a window into what has undoubtedly been a period of great struggle in your child's life, leading you to a posture of compassion rather than anger or disgust, which are all too common emotions that evangelicals have toward gay people. Listening to your child's story doesn't necessarily mean you are fine with a given understanding or decision; it simply recognizes that this is how they are experiencing their life. To negate their story, however, puts them in a place where they are likely to feel they have nowhere to go. Their experience is theirs, not yours.

As part of listening to their story, it is also important to ask them if they are in a relationship or sexually active. It is one thing for a child simply to be dealing with their own attractions and feelings. But once there is another person involved, especially if they are having sex, then that changes things in a big way. Now you are not only dealing with your child's self-awareness, but also with their deep feelings of connection and intimacy to another human. — Brad

When we did talk about your sexual inclinations, it was clearly an issue of tension for you. On the one hand, you had attractions you did not ask for, which you did not choose. On the other hand, you operated on the basis of a worldview inherited from your parents—and at that point embraced by you—which said you could not act on those desires. This is one of those points where it is tempting for me, and probably unwise, to try to do a bit of retroactive psychoanalysis to figure out whether your faith and commitment to the person and ways of Jesus were fundamentally your own, or borrowed from me and Mom.

You and I were so close. You wanted to please me in so many ways. Sometimes in the years that followed, I wondered if your faith was more rooted in your love for me than in an authentic belief of your own. But from what I observed in you, everything in me convinces me to this day that your commitments to and desires for the God of the Bible were authentic and heartfelt. And of course, my mildly Calvinistic leanings have created their own tensions for me on this issue as a theologian. Today you would not identify yourself as a believer in Christ. Theologically speaking, a Calvinist approach to your situation, with its strong emphasis on God's sovereign choosing of the saved and the unsaved, would tend to leave me with one of two conclusions— either your faith in Christ as a young person was fake, or your rejection of the Christ of the Bible now is just an illusion; deep down you still really believe. Unfortunately, while that approach might work at a transcendent level, in the world where the unfathomable and all-knowing God lives, it is simply not satisfying at the level where people live. Where *we* live.

What you believed as a kid, *you really believed.*

And today you don't.

I don't think you are being dishonest about your current lack of faith. One of the most profound things you ever told me was several years ago when you said, "Dad, I really wish I could believe in the faith of my childhood, but I just *can't.*"

DREW

It's true, Dad. And while I had intellectual reasons for leaving the faith, ex-gay "therapy" was a big part of that process for me, emotionally speaking.

I'd like to paraphrase the beach towel you and Mom have at home (the one inscribed with the first page of Jane Austen's *Pride and Prejudice*) by asserting that "it is a truth universally acknowledged that a man who is gay must be in possession of excellent taste."

Working under this stereotypical (but fun!) assumption, it seems ironic that the Stumptown Fellowship, an organization dedicated to helping men overcome their gay "illness," should be housed in one of the most beautiful Craftsman-Victorian homes in Portland's chic Laurelhurst neighborhood. It's almost as if to say, "If you can't have gay love, at least we'll provide you with a *divine* veranda, inlaid Queen Anne floors, and the most *darling* pocket doors you've ever seen." It's the kind of place Jerry Falwell and Liberace could agree on, and the flawless aesthetic environment certainly made my initial visit less intimidating. *I could really get down with this place*, I thought. *Just look at those hand-carved cornices!*

Meeting my counselor, Taylor, however, was a bit disappointing. Small in stature, his chin dressed with a not-quite-successful goatee, he was not the strapping paragon of rough-and-ready masculinity I had hoped for. Where was the Paul Bunyan I had anticipated would lead me, flannel-clad and axe-swinging, into the sunlit woods of fully realized manhood? Taylor did, however, have an excellent sense of humor, and I would laugh a lot in his office over the coming years.

But I would cry more.

The first time I sat down in Taylor's office, I was anxious to show him how much I knew about the ways in which we'd go about fixing this whole homosexual problem. He stopped me right there.

"You don't have to use the word *homosexual* to talk about these struggles, Drew. I use the term Same Sex Attractions—you can call it SSA for short," he smiled. *Thank God*, I thought. *This guy already understands that this is not who I am; it's simply something I'm struggling with. A struggle is something you can win.*

I already knew that I was the youngest client Stumptown Fellowship had ever agreed to take. Now I was going to show them how far ahead of the game I was. Having spent the weeks leading up to our meeting reading everything I could get my hands on relating to ex-gay ideology—both from the internet and from your library at the college—I had come prepared. In short order, I brought Taylor up to speed on the traumatic deficiencies of emotional development I was certain lay at the root of this sexual retardation.

For as long as I can remember, I said, I'd been ignored or tormented by the boys in my life. To the boys at school, at church, on the block, and even among the guys at the after-school drama program, I've landed at various points on the spectrum from incomprehensible "spaz" to ridiculous "faggot." Girls often liked me. Grownups always liked me. But the boys said no. Always no.

While the taunts and cold shoulders were hurtful and annoying, I never used to crave the boys' attention, I told Taylor, until I hit puberty. Before then I wanted the boys to stop picking on me, sure, but it was mostly the girls who I longed to accept me and invite me over to their houses—they were the ones doing the interesting stuff. Like macramé candles. Or playing dress up. Or just talking. Girls understood the value of *talking*! With the boys it was always sports, sports, *sports*. And they were always so sweaty. They *stank*.

Then all at once, I realized that the boys' smell had changed. Or I had changed. Or both had changed. All I knew was that they didn't make me wrinkle my nose anymore. When the boys at school walked by me—especially the guys who were a little older, the athletic ones whose mix of sweat and cologne was strong enough to catch my attention—I felt things I'd never felt before in my stomach. Like butterflies . . . (I mean, of course, they weren't *real* butterflies; *real* butterflies will come when I meet the girl God has planned for me to marry, whereas this is just Satan twisting my brain

"Inappropriate" gender dress-up, 1991.

"Appropriate" gender dress-up, 1998.

chemistry to misfire and confuse me) . . . but yeah, these . . . *fake butterflies*, I guess. And I started to notice their bodies. The boys. I didn't try to! It just kind of happened. And I wanted to be around them. To get to know them and feel like they wanted me around too. There was one of them—this guy two grades above me—who was smart and funny and kind of a bad boy. I realized I wanted to kiss him.

Clearly, without much detective work, we can see what happened here, Taylor, what went wrong along the journey to cause these revolting, unnatural feelings.

Let's eliminate the red herrings, shall we? In my case it's certainly not the father's fault, like it typically is with the male homosexu— sorry, that's right, with *guys who struggle with SSA*. In my case, I have a close relationship with my dad, so it can't be the Absent Father Figure; and even though my mom can be kind of a nag when I don't pick up my clothes, it could hardly be Maternal Over-Attachment. There is a possibility that I was sexually abused by a friend of my parents as a little kid, but we can't confirm this. No, once you rule out the usual suspects the only culprit that's left is also the most obvious answer: failure to bond normally with same-sex peers. While this is less common than Absent Father, Overbearing Mother, or Sexual Abuse (at least from what I've read in the literature, Taylor), it *is* a viable causal agent for SSA, and *basic deductive reasoning* would seem to point the finger there. The years I *should* have spent being socialized by other boys were instead spent being excluded and terrorized by them, and the few friends I had growing up were almost all girls. It's elementary, dear Taylor, elementary school!

There was one exception—Chad, a boy on my street who I used to hang out with all the time. Chad would talk to me about sex. He used to tell me all about the sex his brother had with his girlfriend, and the stuff his brother's girlfriend would let *him* do to her, too. I loved listening to him talk about sex. We used to ride around on our bikes for hours, just me listening to Chad's sex stories, imagining what the two of them looked like doing all that, until his parents divorced and Chad moved away.

So the sources of the cancer seem inescapably clear, Taylor, wouldn't you concur? We're looking at a multi-factorial, dynamic combination of:

1) Failure to initiate Normal Male Gender Bonding, combined with
2) Reversed Female Gender Bonding, combined with
3) Erotically-focused Male Intimacy, all during my formative years, and in a context of
4) Generalized Gender Confusion because . . . because . . . I mean *look* at me!! I *know* how feminine I come across! I hate it. I hate myself for it. I wish I could play sports so I could be with the other guys, the guys at school—to bond with them, I mean. So I could fix this. So I could feel . . . whole, I think.

I just don't know what to do . . . dude.

As I write this book, what I wouldn't give to be a fly on the wall in Taylor's office that day. To watch my twelve-year-old self explain with such confidence the mystery of my sexuality. To my great adolescent relief, I learned that afternoon that we had caught the tumor early. There was, in my case, tremendous hope that I could be cured, at least according to Taylor.

Restoring me to my God-ordained and Christ-centered sense of masculinity wouldn't be a walk in the park; there was much work to be done, and God can only do His miracles in a heart that's humble. But if I was willing to accept the challenge, there was nothing preventing me from beating this and growing into the fully heterosexual man God had designed me to be. It was especially lucky, I learned, that I had come in so early on, what with seventh grade looming on the horizon. Middle school was a crucial time, a make-or-break window for sexual and gender identity development. Because God had led me to Stumptown Fellowship, however, I was already ahead of the perilous curve.

I breathed a sigh of relief.

It was all *fixable*.

I was fixable.

"What about counseling?"

One of the first things many Christian parents think about right away is counseling. Talking with a professional therapist will probably be an important step at some point, for you and for your child, but I encourage you not to rush into it.

If your main agenda for counseling is to simply change your child, you're in trouble. This sentiment will be obvious to your child, and lead to an unproductive counseling experience. Consider having your child get counseling to help them understand and work through their own feelings and concerns. And consider getting counseling for yourself to help you cope with your feelings so you can react in healthier ways. Don't think of it as a silver bullet to "fix" things.

Let me make a brief comment here about ex-gay ministries. Drew has very strong thoughts about this, which I respect, even if I don't agree with him on every point. My observations over the last decade about the effects of ex-gay ministries for same-sex attracted Christian adults are that it is a mixed bag.

The founder of the most well-known ex-gay ministry in Portland, the ministry Drew spent years of his life connected to, is a friend whom I respect. That doesn't mean I agree with all the approaches of ex-gay ministry; I don't. I have talked to many young men who have been through ex-gay programs and for some it has been helpful, for others it has not. The bottom line for me is that the only person who should go to an ex-gay ministry is an adult who understands the process and who really wants help to live out their sexuality in a way that reflects their biblical convictions by participating in a specific program with other men or women who want the same thing. Even then, the process may or may not be helpful.

I have serious concerns about minors being involved in ex-gay therapy. Speaking as clearly as I can, I do not recommend that parents send their children to them. The process deals with deeply rooted emotional and psychological realities which, in the ex-gay ministry context, are often being addressed by people who are not licensed to perform this kind of counseling. It is also personally compelling that the majority of the professional psychological community thinks ex-gay ministry for minors is a really bad idea. Further, evidence indicates that the likelihood of attempted suicide for LGBTQ young people is exacerbated by ex-gay therapy.

There is a fundamental difference between a thirty-year-old going to ex-gay therapy of his own volition and a thirteen-year-old sent by his parents. Honestly, I have not always held this view. I hold it now, in part, because ex-gay ministry was a damaging experience for Drew; he was too young, and part of his motivation for going was because I wanted him to. —Brad

BRAD

Your seventh grade year found you at a Christian middle school. We figured you would be comfortable there, having grown up in the church with your dad as a pastor.

There were some great moments there. I will always be thankful for an English and Drama teacher who saw more than a boy who didn't fit in, who saw your bright mind, your unusually advanced understanding of theater and fashion, and your great sense of humor. She invested in you, pressed you to stretch yourself academically, and in the spring, instead of directing the school play herself, she allowed you to do it. Just the other day, over a decade later, a friend said to me, "Do you remember when Drew directed *Hillbilly Hankerin'*?" This teacher believed in you and you did something really memorable.

But it didn't bring the connection with other boys we hoped for; some friendships showed early promise, but fizzled.

From a teacher . . .

When fourteen-year-old Drew auditioned for our church theater production, I never could have imagined what was in store. When he began to sing, I put down my pencil and could not look away.

Thus began a friendship, mentorship, and family connection that continued with Drew as my student in his high school choir and musicals. Over the years, Drew looked to me as not just a teacher, but as a mentor and, at times, a parent.

When Drew told me that he was gay, to be truthful, I didn't know how to respond. I had never experienced such a disclosure

from a friend, let alone a student. I'm from a kind and loving but very conservative Christian background. Based on
our faith, there was zero tolerance for prejudice or wrongful
treatment of anyone. But growing up, prejudice or judgment
for us referred to race, not sexuality. I can't remember even
discussing it.

After our talk, I remember crying and asking God to please
work in Drew's heart, to change him into something I was
more comfortable with. Let him be lazy, let him be unmoti-
vated, let him be angry, let him be . . . anything but gay.

One evening before he left for NYC, he came over to my house
to chat again. I felt frustrated as we talked in the kitchen. He was
defensive, trying as hard as he could to get me to agree with "his
side." He challenged me as I feebly tried to offer my opinion
in an area that I really didn't know much about. I felt cornered,
and in anger I finally shouted, "What is it you want me to
say, Drew?" He wanted me to tell him that he and his future
partner would be welcome to come into my home, eat dinner

together, and stay here overnight.
For me to accept them coming to
stay at my house just as I would
if his partner was a woman. I told
him I could not do that. Then I
said such a hurtful statement it
grieves me to repeat my words. I
said that the very thought of Drew
in bed with another man made me
physically ill.

As I remember that awful moment,
I can see the look on his face. It
rips my heart. He left.

State Choir Competition, 2005.

After about a year of silence, Drew sent me a brief email from New York, reopening a door I feared I had closed. "Things are hard for us right now," he said. "I am experiencing a lot of pain working out who I am in the context of my past and my future. What I want you to know is that I love you, and that you are more important to me than I can say. I hope we will be able to talk soon. I miss you. You will never stop being a part of my life."

I thanked him for reminding me that the love was still there. I felt it too. "I pray each day for you," I assured him, "for happiness, and fulfillment, for good health, God's protection, and with gratitude for what you have added to my life. I also pray each day for myself—for understanding, for compassion and clarity. I believe that you and I will always be connected by love, even if we are not able to stand together on our beliefs. You will always be 'my Drew'—please don't ever doubt it again."

It was Christmastime, two years later, when I was finally able to address the rift that had been wedged between us back in my kitchen on that spring afternoon. "Drew, I want to tell you some things that have been very heavy on my heart," I wrote him. "I know that we are not on the same page in regards to your life choices, and I know I have hurt you with some of my comments. I want to correct that. I will never forget the evening in my kitchen when we had an extremely disturbing conversation, and you told me you wanted me to accept your lifestyle. I felt cornered by your persistence and your demanding request. I remember telling you then, as is still true, that I feel confused and torn about the entire homosexual situation. I want you to know, however, that I understand that the way I gave my reply was hurtful. I should not have expressed my anxiety the way I did. All you heard was rejection. I am very, very sorry that I said those words. In spite of my continuing struggle to come to grips with this complex issue, I pray that I will always be compassionate, loving, and accepting of everyone, especially you. I hope you will accept my apology, as well as my continuing attempt to understand the complexity of your life. You will always be so special to me."

I don't think I am alone here. Other adults in similar positions have said hurtful things, things they will regret and wish they could retract. If such words are said, time helps, and extra doses of grace, patience, and love help, verbalizing unconditional acceptance and the kind of value that we all need from those we trust and look up to. We each have the privilege of offering our hand to these beautiful teens who turn to us as their confidant and a provider of hope in this complicated life. —Jeanette

In fact, as I look back, I believe your years in a Christian school may have been the beginning of the end of your sense of belonging in the Church. Here you were in this environment where so many of the basic theological and biblical ideas were familiar, and at that time, largely comfortable to you. Yet you also began to see that you did not fit, began to feel that there may not be a place for you. But you still kept trying.

DREW

It's hard work recalling these years of my "therapy" at Stumptown Fellowship, because God and human evolution saw fit to equip our brains with trauma suppression. There are different kinds of trauma: some trauma is physical, other trauma is psychological; some trauma is acute, like rape, while other trauma simmers over time, like an emotionally abusive marriage, or a Phish concert. For me, ex-gay therapy falls into the last two categories: psychological trauma that simmers slowly. Over years.

I usually have to revisit the printed literature of the ex-gay movement, or my old journals, in order to even remember what I talked about at Stumptown Fellowship, otherwise my brain draws a blank. Some demons have to be *summoned*.

There are a few things that I will never quite be able to suppress, though, like the moment in eighth grade when Taylor informed me, his smiling face full of wisdom and compassion, that a rather unremarkable sexual fantasy I had experienced in a dream involving me and another boy was something much more troubling. This dream, Taylor assured me, was nothing less than my subconscious expressing *cannibalism*. My twisted desire, he told me, once the dream was properly interpreted, was to consume the other boy, to *eat* him.

"Like Jeffrey Dahmer?" I asked.

"That's an extreme example," he replied, "but the principle is the same."

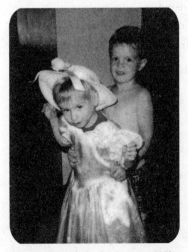

"Inappropriate" gender dress-up, 1992.

"Appropriate" gender dress-up, 1993.

At the time of this writing, I have never captured, raped, murdered, dismembered, refrigerated, and eaten any little boys like Jeffrey Dahmer was fond of doing. Really, in today's fast-paced world, who has that kind of time? But when I was thirteen years old, my trusted ex-gay "therapist" assured me that my common wet dream revealed that this evil lurked deep inside me—that my attractions, if followed to their endpoint, would warp me into an unthinkable demon.

This, it's safe to say, was damaging.

Today, my sexuality is intertwined with all manner of abjection, internalized hate, and self-destructive instincts. The kind of sweet, easy intimacy that many of my gay friends have with their significant others is something I have only rarely known. When it does seem to come along, my brain tells me, *That's not FOR you, because you are broken and twisted. Remember, your desire to be physically intimate with him is the same desire as a serial killer.* When those kinds of messages are ingrained so deeply in a child, dismantling them as an adult is neither simple nor quick.

Ex-gay ideology says my intimacy problems today are the result of my "brokenness" as a practicing homosexual (I always giggle at the term "practicing," as though homosexuality were like playing Rachmaninoff, or podiatry; do you get better at it as you practice? Do you need a license?) The vast majority of psychological research and opinion, on the other hand, would say that my sexual hang-ups are the result of "therapy" that was actually a kind of long-term trauma which forced a twelve-to-seventeen-year-old kid to internalize only ugly, self-loathing, and destructive ideas about himself as a sexual being.

Whose fault is it that I experienced this?

Plenty of people from my world would say unequivocally that

it's yours and Mom's for taking me there, Dad, but I disagree; you and Mom were loving parents who had no idea the kinds of things that were being said to your child behind closed doors. The perpetrator was an insidious system of thought within conservative Christian culture that equated same-sex love with every predatory, inhuman, and fearsome behavior.

Perhaps the most shattering moment in this slow, quiet hell came as a result of my first sexual experience with another boy.

In seventh grade, there was a guy in the class above me with a goofy grin and green eyes. Around the end of the year, a rumor emerged that he'd admitted to being bisexual. In the final week of classes this whisper swirled around our halls (okay, *hall*—we only had the one, but it could swirl juicy tidbits like a hall twice its size because Christian middle-schoolers can *gossip*; there were just so few gang fights and unplanned pregnancies, we had to work with what we had).

When I first heard the rumor I was surprised, because he was a jock. He didn't strike me as the type to suffer from my disease. I began speculating on his home life, his relationship to his parents, whether he'd ever been sexually abused, trying as best I could to fit him into the ex-gay psychological schema I'd been working to master. These diligent field notes were far from my mind, however, the night of the eighth grade graduation house party.

Any Christian parent worth their salt knows that nothing good can come from a house party. It's part of the Evangelical Parenting Creed, right between "What goes in your ears comes out your mouth" and "Pet your dog, not your date." House Parties are dens of iniquity where drugs, sex, alcohol, sex, R-rated movies, sex, rap-music-that-isn't-Macklemore, and *sex* all come together in a perfect storm of unsupervised temptation. And sex. But church youth group can only happen so many nights a week, so—outside of total house arrest—usually all the parents can do is drop the kids off, have a frantic conversation with the hosting child's parents, and hope to God the family isn't wealthy enough to have an unsupervised guesthouse.

The night of our eighth grade graduation, there was definitely a guesthouse.

Free from parental eyes, we Christian seventh and eighth graders let loose in unmitigated debauchery: mixed-gender Ping Pong tournaments, backyard BB gun shenanigans, and unconscionable amounts of soda consumption. It was practically *Animal House*. At one point, wildly disinhibited after a fifth Mountain Dew, someone brought up the subject of the sexuality of the boy in question. He brazenly admitted that he was bi, and I was floored.

I saw him anew. *How brave*, I thought, *to admit this in public. What cojones.* I suddenly noticed his height, the athletic bulk of his body. My stomach started doing somersaults.

Soon, the lights of the guesthouse dimmed. We were all watching a horror movie. I sat on the couch next to the boy. With the delicacy of a dragonfly and the measured slowness of Mr. Miyagi, I let my foot carefully brush against his until he slowly brushed back. I thrilled with terror. This went on for what felt like forever, until something in my guts thickened, and I got up from the couch, catching his eye as I made my way outside into the summer night. He followed.

There was a series of questions, asked by me, answered by him. I walked back and forth across the poured concrete patio along the side of the guesthouse, my hands clasped behind my back, my brow feverish, swerving only fitfully to look at him. He stood still, his tall, lazy figure leaned against the corrugated garage door cool as could be in the yellow glow of the floodlight. The scene looked like a Nazi commandant interrogating his prisoner.

How long had he known of these feelings? I demanded he tell me the precise nature of his homosexual attractions; how were they different from his attractions to girls? I wanted *details*. I let flow a rapid-fire analysis of my own experience with the disease, why I suffered from it, how I planned to cure it.

"It's natural," he said. "There's nothing wrong with it. If it wasn't natural you wouldn't want it."

"But what about God?"

"I don't really believe in God. Not like that, anyway."

And then it was over. Once the Divine Judge had been banished into the darkness by the words of this older boy, there was only our bodies, and how it felt to bring them together. Granted, it might have been more romantic to fool around somewhere other than inside a musty canoe against the back of the guesthouse, but it was still an explosive pleasure I had never known before. Then, as quick as it started, it was done. You and Mom picked me up at the end of the night. I went to bed like nothing had happened.

But everything was different.

As a kid, I was never any good at holding a guilty secret. I would try, and before long my tender soul would acquire the toxicity of W.C. Fields' late career liver. I'm not sure how long it took me before I broke down in full confession to Taylor, but it was probably within a week. He was comforting in his assurance that nothing I could ever do would separate me from the gracious forgiveness of Jesus, but stern in his diagnosis that I had now crossed a line. My body had known sin.

It was incumbent upon me, he said gently, to tell you and Mom. With expansive benevolence, Taylor said it would be no problem for me to tell you both in his office during my next session. He let you know that your presence was requested the following week, but left it a mystery as to what the reason might be.

Over the following days, the tension in our house was palpable. As always, the three conspirators—you, me, and Mom—took pains to make it seem that nothing was the matter, so as not to spook the horses. I'm sure we thought we did a great job of hiding all this from the "kids," a delusion I labored under until a few years ago when little brother Corey informed me that even at the tender age of seven, "I always knew there was s*** going down. Duh. You guys really thought you were subtle. You weren't."

It was an early evening the day before our scheduled meeting when you called me out onto the porch. The sinking sun lit up the massive cedar trees in our backyard, and you were sitting in a green plastic deck chair, your face a furrowed mask of pain, and an emotion I had only seen you wear once before—fear. My stomach dropped.

"There's something I have to ask you before we go into our meeting tomorrow," you said.

He knows. My mind raced. *He knows what happened. He's going to ask and I'm going to have to tell him.*

I tried to steel myself against terrified resignation. There is no hiding from the Lord as He walks through Eden in the cool of the evening. You would ask me if I had eaten the apple, and I would have to say "yes." And there was no Eve, no Serpent to pass the blame onto. Just me and my sin.

"Does what you have to tell us tomorrow . . . ," you paused, closing your eyes for an instant before turning to face me. " . . . does what you have to talk to us about tomorrow have anything to do with children?"

It took me a second to realize what you were asking.

But then it dawned on me.

I'll never forget that moment.

My first sexual experience itself wasn't what would haunt me; it was your *reaction* to it that broke my heart and left me reeling for years.

> The false stereotype of gay people being pedophiles or child abusers is one of the most common and damaging myths about us in circulation.
>
> Child abuse in any context whatsoever is absolutely wrong. There is no credible study that links homosexuality with pedophilia. Many child abusers are in fact heterosexual in their adult sexual relations. A correlation between gay people and pedophiles is not only unsupportable scientifically, it is enraging and simply wrong for a gay person to be suspected of such a thing with no other basis than their sexual orientation. —**Drew**

The *fear* on your face—the emotion I had only ever seen on the day you returned from having been kidnapped by a schizophrenic member of the church you pastored who told you he was going to kill you before you escaped out of his moving car—this *abject terror* was because you feared your son was a pedophile. A *predator*. You were so afraid, in fact, that you couldn't wait another twenty-four hours to know.

At that moment, something inside me died, and was never again alive after that. If my own father, the man who knew me better than anyone on earth, who loved me and saw all the ways in which I strove to emulate my parents' goodness, could be so terrified that I had preyed on one of the beautiful and innocent children with whom I was often entrusted . . . what did that mean for me?

What kind of monster am I? What the hell is wrong with me?

BRAD

I hate conflict, and when it comes up I want it dealt with right away. Having to wait to resolve a difficult situation with someone I love is like being sent to the principal's office only to be told to sit and wait for him to deal with me in an hour.

So when you told us you had something serious to talk to Mom and me about, but that it would have to wait until your next appointment with your ex-gay counselor, it was *torture*. I ran through half-a-dozen scenarios, even wondering—and I say this to my shame now—if you had possibly sexually abused one of the kids you were babysitting. Worse, I asked you about that even before we went to the appointment. You were horrified and deeply hurt. I was relieved, while also sorry that my assumption was so painful for you. Only later did I realize that I had made the same destructive, wrong assumption so many conservative straight people do—quietly believing the lie that if you are gay, you are probably also a pedophile.

When we finally had the meeting with your counselor, you told us about the graduation party and the bisexual boy. I can only imagine how his revelation must have hit you. Around you were students who were appalled, disgusted, but going through your mind, I'm sure, was something like, "Dear God! I'm not alone!" So far all this was no big deal, but then you dropped the bomb—this boy's public announcement led to your first sexual experience.

My initial response was not one of anger, disappointment, or despair. Rather, I would describe it as carefully controlled panic. After all, I was a former pastor in an evangelical church. I was a theologian at an evangelical college, known by hundreds of students who looked to me as an example of a well-lived Christian life. *How will what Drew's done reflect on me?*

Thank God those self-centered thoughts were fleeting.

This was not about me. It was about you—my son.

What would conservative Christian America have me do at this point? I wondered. Lock you in your room and homeschool you until you were eighteen? Hang posters with all the passages from the Bible that condemn homosexuality? Make you sit with me every night and watch Arnold Schwarzenegger movies and macho westerns (minus *Brokeback Mountain*) to get you to see the attraction of being ruggedly heterosexual?

I was a mess. And to be honest, I did not seek much counsel, especially from evangelicals. Most of what I had received there had been ignorant, overly simplistic, and, at worst, *damaging* stuff. So I just decided to wrap my arms around you and keep walking together, hoping that our closeness and your faith in God would give you what you needed to see the journey through, to follow God's call in your life from the Bible as I understood it.

But I knew you needed someone else, someone to walk with you who understood your struggles firsthand.

Fortunately, I knew just the right person.

Chapter Four

WITH A LITTLE HELP FROM MY FRIENDS

BRAD

Alex was bright, culturally savvy, loved art and literature, and was as fashionable a dresser as Clinton from *What Not to Wear.* His sexual attraction issues were similar to yours. He loved Jesus and wanted to follow Him through his struggles, and he was engaged to a sweet, supportive woman named Hannah, who I knew, along with Alex, would *love* you. I asked Alex if he would be willing to talk with you. He agreed, with both joy and concern, knowing that walking with you on your pilgrimage would be another version of facing the brutality of his own.

It was a Saturday morning. I walked with you up to the door of the house called "Aslan's How," owned by one of my colleagues at the college and decorated in the theme of C.S. Lewis's *Chronicles of Narnia* children's fantasy series. I knew you would be comfortable there—and with Alex.

DREW

"Aslan's How" is one of those things that only other evangelicals can understand. I have tried to explain to friends from outside our subculture about the fraternity of weirdo intellectuals who lived in Dr. Friesen's Narnia-themed cottage, where every room was decorated to evoke a particular episode of C.S. Lewis's beloved *Chronicles* that all Christian children grow up on. The looks I get from them range from dumbly confused to unpleasantly suspicious. Explain Aslan's How to someone from an evangelical background, however—someone who doesn't need to be told that Aslan is the giant talking lion who represents Jesus in the Narnia world—and I'll feel the thrill of shared community experience, like when a stranger on the subway joins in the chorus to an Amy Grant song I'm humming. There are swords on the walls! Vintage Narnian chess sets! A real-live wardrobe *that you can walk through!* (There's a closet on the other side. With a lamppost and fake snow.)

Pulling up to the How, we went to the back door (the one that takes you through the Underworld tunnel Prince Rilian falls down in *The Silver Chair*). A young man answered the door. The first thing I noticed about him was his hair, dyed a rebelliously ruddy brown, obscuring one of his shy, sensitive eyes. I couldn't tell if his haircut was Neo-Classic-Emo or Emo-Revivalist, but it was definitely working.

I had wondered so much about what this potential savior would be like: would he be the Jock-for-Jesus type? Would he be fat and ugly? Would he be young and hot? How masculine or feminine would his demeanor be? Would I be turned on by him, or repulsed? Would he be everything I longed to become, or everything I was trying to escape?

I had been steeled for anything, but what I couldn't have

expected was *Alex*. Alex the witty. Alex the cynical. Alex the shy, understated expert on indie, secular subculture—music, film, and television that were levels of cool I hadn't *dreamed* of till then. Alex, who brought Sufjan Stevens and *Arrested Development* and hipster coffee into my pimply, suburban high school universe, rendering me instantly cooler than I had a right to be. Alex, who spent hours driving me around misty, moody Portland in his white early-90s Mazda truck, wearing offensively stylish leather driving gloves. I can still remember how he smelled, full of wool and leather and the strange, musty-sour scent of that stupid truck. His scent was more human than masculine *per se*; there was nothing erotic in it, but everything comforting.

Alex and I got on immediately, like we'd known each other our whole lives. Becoming his friend was a turning point. For the first time in my life there was another man whose mere *existence* made me feel less alone. The isolation of my suffering was entered by another person—another guy! A Christian guy who wasn't ugly or insipid, who was hip and weird and wonderful! The many mornings we spent at coffee before church were full of uncensored and hilarious repartee that I had never known with anyone other than you, Dad.

Alex sometimes took me to Prokope meetings (*prokope* is Greek for "progress"), the group you helped lead where young Christian men from your university got together to support each other in their "sexual brokenness." While that meant something different for everyone, and while in theory I appreciated the chance to normalize myself by sharing my struggles in the context of other Christian males' attempts to live biblically, the experience of sitting around in a circle listening to these dudes talk about their battles with masturbation and straight porn was not my cup of tea. I always felt, deep inside, that no matter how warm and welcoming they were, they still saw me as a freak, albeit one to whom they were obligated to show compassion and understanding, seeing as I was *your* son.

But being with Alex was worth the awkward moments. When I became a big enough part of his life for him to introduce me to his fiancée, Hannah, I was relieved to meet a woman who wasn't threatened by me, who loved me like a little brother. When they got married, I was delighted and relieved because I knew that they were two people meant to be together. I believed then, as I do now, that their male and female genders were correct *incidentally*; it was Alex and Hannah's *souls* that were mated, irrespective of their biblically sanctioned hetero sex organs. This seemed a miracle, and I was sure that God had provided it; certainly, there was hope for me too.

In the years to follow, as I began to experience what would become my great unraveling, I was always open and honest with Alex about the growing doubts I wrestled with. I knew he and Hannah cared for me no matter what. This young Christian couple wanted to be with me, to spend authentic and loving time together even as I became less and less certain about what I believed.

So for a long time, Alex was The Great Ex-Gay Hope. He was the older brother I had always yearned for, a male friend who understood my battles. Alex was farther enough ahead of me down the path of victorious suffering to offer genuine hope, but close enough to my stage in life to feel like a travel buddy, not a pedagogue. I was grateful for him, and so happy you introduced us.

Years later, however, once Alex moved to Boston to attend Harvard and my homosexuality had become something I defended as ferociously as I had once attempted to conceal and cure it, I came to hold Alex in the deepest possible contempt, to resent him with a vitriol that was frightening. It was because of what I thought he represented. Alex had been the brother I had loved and leaned on—but he was also the son you should have had. The son I failed to be. The son who was *strong* enough, *righteous* enough, *man* enough to  fix his problem, marry a woman, and produce a son of his own. My jealousy and self-loathing for my inability to do the same was more than I could bear, and I decided that I would never speak to Alex and Hannah again. When I heard, while living in New York, that their toddler son had gotten cancer, my reaction was smug. I was viciously glad to hear that the product of Alex's Christ-approved sexuality was somehow "defective." The living proof of Alex's victory over his "broken" sexuality was revealed to be, itself, a broken trophy. *What poetic justice*, I gloated. My bitterness was happy to hear of his tragedy, my bitterness that resented all the longing and disappointment that Alex's son—whom I had never met—represented for me in my failed attempts to become what you'd wanted for me.

I was horrified by these feelings. How could I feel satisfaction over the tragedy befalling an innocent child, who had nothing to do with my own pain? How could I feel vindicated at the suffering of his parents, two people who had loved me and treasured me for exactly who I was, regardless of what I would come to believe?

How wicked is my heart? I wondered.

Who cares, a crueler part of me thought. *They deserve it.*

Stop that! You're sick and inhuman!

And they represent everything that's inhumanly oppressive about the world you finally freed yourself from! It's the beliefs of people like them that make gay kids throw themselves off bridges and in front of moving cars.

That's so unfair. They're good people! You're gloating in the suffering of an innocent child!

And on and on, until I found it easier to simply put the situation out of my mind.

This internal battle is the kind of thing that happens when hated systems intersect with cherished individuals. Those kinds of maelstroms of the heart and mind follow two separate logics at once. Meaningful resolution isn't really possible, because battles like this don't really make sense in the first place. They're just awful.

But on the day you dropped me off at the door of Narnia, these frightening feelings were years ahead of me. Back in those days, Alex was nothing short of the Godsend I'd been waiting for. Maybe now, finally, I would start to experience the healing that Stumptown Fellowship had been promising. I was doing my part; the rest was up to God.

It was just a matter of time.

BRAD

For several years, you found yourself able to navigate between your commitment to God and an evangelical Christian lifestyle on the one hand, and a powerful attraction to boys on the other. Interestingly, one of the realities that empowered you to live in that tension was a woman—Andrea.

You were a freshman when you told us about her. "Mom, Dad, this girl is *amazing*! She is beautiful and intelligent. She loves literature and philosophy. For goodness sake, she has read the *Great Books of the Western World!*"

I remember the day I met Andrea at Starbucks. She was everything you said she was—beautiful and smart, with a heart of gold. More than that, she was strong and stubborn enough to be your match at every point. On the one hand, when the two of

A few years into the self-conversion attempt. Note the 2003-vintage cool-guy outfit and bro posture.

you started dating, Mom and I were a bit concerned—you were so young. But then there was the fact that she was a *girl*! We were cautiously hopeful. Could this relationship give you the hope you needed to believe that you could find joy and fulfillment in a woman—the very thing we believed God wanted for you?

DREW

The wonderful thing about Andrea was that, at the core of our relationship, she was never my "solution" and she was never my "beard"—gay slang for a woman whom a closeted man dates or marries to hide his sexuality (MGM and Universal Studios used to have battalions of young leggy "beards" on hand for this purpose, sworn to secrecy and contracted to appear in public alongside all the old silver-screen heroes Grandma and Granddad still think were straight). While you and Mom were overjoyed to see me dating a girl, I was just incredulous that there was another person in my sub-urban evangelical world who wanted to talk about the implications of Rousseau's philosophy for the American nationalist project. This was a *major* development.

What I found in this superb young lady was a tremendous friend. She could make me laugh like nobody else could. We were at once fully committed to Christ and mischievously cynical about the earthly church. Andrea and I could lead youth group worship team together with authentic abandon, then spend the rest of the evening lampooning the ridiculousness of "Christian" gender politics or the secret hypocrisy of Church Ladies, cruising around in her beater red convertible with the duct-taped top.

We fought constantly, which was sexy. Back then, before my sense of sexual identity had become calcified by a pugnacious hatred for ex-gay and the socio-political imperatives of what it would mean to "come out," my sexual attraction to Andrea had the romance and curiosity of a barely post-pubescent boy. I became naturally, sexually aware of this other person with whom I shared such an easy bond, and with whom I spent so much time. Sexual experimentation, however, was not on the table for a girl like Andrea, who was committed—with the airtight assurance of a whip-smart alpha female raised in a patriarchal society, the kind of girl who reads the score long before the men start to notice her—to sexual abstinence until marriage. Any attempts I made at breaching that wall were gently, but firmly, rebuffed.

This didn't bother me. If I had been your typical heterosexual ball of raging adolescent hormones, I might have been more upset. But since my unruly sexuality had already been designated a hazard to my health, body, and soul, it was nice to be with a girl who allowed me to repress it as much as I knew it needed to be. When I finally told her that I was in therapy to help me rid myself of unwanted homosexual attractions, and used my best ex-gay logic to explain the causes of this pesky but fixable bump in the road, Andrea took it as the calm, pragmatic person she was. It seemed almost a non-issue.

"So, you're not disgusted with me?" I asked her.

"Of course not," she said. "Why would I be? I love you for exactly who you are. This is part of you, you're doing what you have to do to deal with it, and I love you as I always have. Even more so for telling me. It's extremely brave. I'm proud of you."

That was Andrea.

No nonsense, totally sure about those she loved. I felt so lucky to have a friend like her, and I had no trouble imagining us continuing, just as we were, until the right time for marriage came along and we'd be officially grafted into each other's families, parents who already loved the other's kid as if we were their own. Andrea and I were each other's best friend, just like you and Mom.

BRAD

For a couple of years, Andrea was like another member of our family. The scary question for your mom and me was, *what would she do when she found out?* Well, the night you laid your cards on the table, Andrea's response was one of grace and true friendship. She already had come to love you for who you were. The fact that you had same sex attractions did not change that.

It was a powerful moment for you. This person who was so much a part of the evangelical Christian culture accepted you for who you were. At that point in time (and still today), evangelicals did not talk about homosexuality much, except to condemn it, so the fact that she still wanted to move forward in your relationship was profound.

When I think about your dating relationship with Andrea,

however, I know that it was filled with significant strain. On the one hand, you truly loved her. The two of you laughed, you argued, and you talked about things that mattered. But at the same time your attraction to boys was always there, pulling you in another direction. Your relationship with Andrea did not diminish it, your faith did not crush it, your prayers did not deliver you from it, and ex-gay counseling did not cure it.

DREW

When asked what he believed in during an interview, I remember Woody Allen answering that he believed in "the power of distraction." How true that is; distraction can get us through life's ugliness, mundanity, and injustices, and laughter is one of the best forms of distraction—both for its pleasure and its effectiveness.

Laughter was something Andrea and Alex and I had plenty of. For years, its power, combined with the approval of a community that celebrated my friendship with a wonderful guy and my courtship with a wonderful girl, was enough to make those two authentic friendships into the stopgap I needed.

Prince   Bride

But it couldn't last forever.

I truly loved Andrea, and I truly loved Alex. But I had yet to ever truly fall in love.

"A perfect wedding"—Drew's favorite drawing from his cousin, 1992.

Chapter Five

TAKE ME
TO CHURCH

BRAD

During these early high school years, church was a mixed blessing for you. You were *so* glad to finally move beyond middle school, hoping to hang out with kids whose reading choices transcended *The Magic Tree House* or the *Left Behind* series. You couldn't wait to go to summer camp with the boys, each year hoping *this* would be the year when you made friendships with guys that would last beyond the week. And sure as the changing of the seasons, each year you came home and told us what a blast you had—singing, listening to the camp speaker, playing crazy games—and also about one or two boys whom you thought you *really* bonded with that year.

Then weeks went by.

The phone never rang for you.

As a dad, what can someone say to a boy who is smart, talented, funny, loved by the girls, but mostly shut out by boys year after year? The hopes I harbored that high school boys at church would finally "get you" eventually turned into one of my lamest mantras: "Don't worry, Drew. College students are much more mature and diverse in their interests. They will get you." But I think by then you had begun to lose faith in my assurances. I had too.

As you came into your own as a member of the evangelical subculture, you became acutely aware that this subculture is tied together not only by belief, but by a very strong code of conduct. And by the time you are in high school that code begins to address the issue of sex.

Perhaps there is no place more uncomfortable on the entire earth for a high schooler than the Christian youth group sex talk. Sometimes, if these talks are general, they include both genders. But when they get to . . . *specifics* . . . they traditionally break into boys' and girls' groups to discuss the more intimate issues of sexuality. Most Christian kids joke about sex in the schoolyard, but to have to listen to an adult talk about "it" makes every minute seem like an eternity. The idea of actually raising your hand and asking a question is about as attractive as having your teeth drilled without Novocain.

"My child wants to come out at church. Should I let him?"

Sadly, you should be cautious here, at least early on. You need to do some quiet legwork first to at least have an idea of what your child will face.

If this seems healthy, it would be good to have him talk to a youth pastor first. Drew's experience with that was very good. His youth pastor responded to Drew with love and grace and took him to breakfast regularly for some time, really just for the purpose of listening and to communicate to Drew that theirs was a safe relationship. To this day Drew feels a deep love and respect for that pastor, even though the direction Drew ultimately went was not what that pastor would have chosen for Drew. On the other hand, coming out, say, on Facebook for all their youth group friends to see will likely create the kind of polarization social media is famous for—and end up more hurtful than helpful.

In my conversations with evangelical pastors—especially youth pastors—over the last few years, I have met many who are moving away from quick reactions to gay church members and working to listen, understand, and offer guidance and community. I need to say that this kind of posture can happen regardless of how conservative one's theology of sexuality may be. If you have this kind of pastor, a visit with them could be helpful. If not, a pastoral visit might produce little more than increased self-hatred for your kid and a growing resolution to disconnect from the church. In the latter case, be patient, and search and pray for an "Alex." —**Brad**

I never attended one of these talks with you. I know how they are because I had to endure them as a kid myself. But in your case, these talks held an added element of discomfort.

I doubt the youth group sex talks at our church were of a particularly gay-bashing variety, but I'm also sure they clearly communicated the assumption that sex and marriage were meant by God to be between a man and a woman. Your own agonizing awareness that this was not how your attractions were shaped made these sessions little more than exercises in self-condemnation.

I remember one night in our family room during these early high school years when you told me with deep sadness, "Dad, I could never tell the boys in the youth group about my sexual attractions. If I did I would be immediately cut off." How ironic that at the very time you were so desperate for male peers who would just hang out with you and enjoy you for who you were, the last person you felt you could be was *yourself*.

> As a Christian theologian and former pastor, one of my greatest frustrations is that, at least when it comes to sexuality, it is often safer for a young person to be honest at the public school than it is at church, a place that is meant to be driven by love and grace, a community where people walk with each other. No matter what. —Brad

DREW

Recently, Dad, you and I were on our way to Gramma's house on the rural outskirts of town riding in "Basic Bob," your old red truck unburdened by radio, air conditioning, power steering, or cup holders. As a kid we drove that route a million times, not to go to Gramma's but to go to church, the sprawling campus nestled in a quiet wetland where the clustered strip malls and housing developments of suburbia taper into the farmhouses that once characterized the outer county. As we pulled off the I-205 freeway I asked you, without warning, if we could go see it. I hadn't been in years.

There's really no place more jam-packed with memories for me than that church campus. My old high school doesn't come close. Pulling into the massive parking lot of asphalt and gravel, I could feel myself shifting internally the way I sometimes do when I'm entering a Christian setting: my eyes harden, I feel my stomach lurch and my jaw clench, and my closed-mouth smile gets set in rubbery place—it's the only time I'm sphinxlike. Noticing the internal clockwork falling into place, however, I stopped. I decided to *breathe*.

Relax, I told myself. *Just chill. Let your heart be open.*

I got out of the truck. The sun was bright in the parking lot, hanging directly overhead in the kind of cloudless blue sky we get throughout the perfect Portland summers. The air was extremely still.

I inhaled my surroundings slowly, and saw ghosts everywhere.

There, in place of an empty parking lot, were the giant yellow buses lined up two and three at a time, ready to be filled with sunburnt middle and high schoolers damp with new sweat and the sticky remnants of whatever lake or freezing Pacific bay we'd been swimming in that afternoon. I saw Sharon, the church custodian and do-it-all everywoman (an accomplished taxidermist and the only other person I've ever met who was conversant in the elvish language from *The Lord of the Rings*), wrapping hundreds of sandwiches with her rough bronzed hands, cackling at some teenage gossip. Foxtails and Frisbees and footballs soared above the freshly mowed grass, and the playground was alive with "carpet ball," that game played with billiard balls in a long, carpeted trough, which I'm not sure is a real game anywhere outside of Christian summer camps.

Best part of summer—
Vacation Bible School, 1993.

Standing there, watching the visions in the parking lot, I was happy. The cold recrimination I'd steeled myself for was absent, replaced by warm nostalgia.

How lucky was I to have experienced a childhood like this?

Yeah, sure, I was always pining for an acceptance I would never really get, some holy grail of testosterone-filled bonding dangled over me by ex-gay ideology, but so what? There were so many people in my life who loved me, these warm-hearted Christians who made me a part of the world they built for us kids! So what if they were all grownups and girls?

Standing there now, from the vantage point of a twenty-six-year-old man whose life overflows with the male "buddy" relationships I had yearned for back then, I wished I could transmit a message to my thirteen-year-old self through space-time: *It's going to be fine! You're going to grow up to like who you are, and have fulfilling relationships of all kinds! Don't waste breath berating yourself for not having the "right" kinds of friendships! It's all good, kid. It's going to be okay.*

Staring out across the empty fields toward the church offices, I saw a small blonde figure sitting in the shade of the porch on one of the cheap plastic tragedies that pass for church deck furniture. I knew who it was right away. You and I walked over to see Scott, my old youth pastor.

I'm not sure what it is with Christian youth pastors, but they could make a fortune selling it on Rodeo Drive and Madison Avenue, because these men NEVER GET OLD. They look exactly the same. For decades, I've heard "Black Don't Crack," and I know the Chinese have secrets too (Dad, your Sino-American sister-in-law is the only woman in her Laguna Beach gated community who's never had a lift or tuck but looks the same today as she did in '93), but among white people the only ones who can bypass all physical signs of aging sans Botox are youth pastors. Perhaps it's the games they play, the silly camp songs they sing, or the ebullient love they have for God and His children that keeps the wrinkles at bay, but, sure enough, Scott was just as I remembered him, though I hadn't seen his rosy smiling face in ages.

After hugs and greetings, Scott and I walked around the church campus catching up and laughing. In high school we'd spent a lot of time together, what with all the leadership work I did over the years, and we met regularly for Saturday morning coffee for quite a spell. In those years before I had a driver's license, you would drop me at "Cafe D'Vine," the coffee shop run by our rival suburban megachurch across the highway, and connected to the Christian bookshop "Branches" (these two shops' names were a reference to Jesus's words, "I am the Vine and you are the Branches"; just the kind of cutesy Christian kitsch that makes you cringe but makes me wet my pants with joy, like a Thomas Kinkade coffee mug, or those T-shirts with pictures of brush, toothpaste, and floss, that read "Brushing up on God's Word prevents Truth Decay").

Morning coffee at Cafe D'Vine was always pretty chill. Scott's an unassuming guy if ever there was one, easygoing and ready to laugh, your "basic Christian dude" who's gifted for that most millennial of evangelical axioms, "Just tryna love people right where they're at." Here was a guy who'd easily be written off by my sophisticated New York gay friends as a Christian simpleton who should be pitied for investing his life in "ministry" (whatever that is!) and disparaged for the kind of "judgment and self-hatred" he *must* have instilled in the gay youth *trapped* in his suburban *Christianity*.

And yet that's not how I remember Scott at all.

Any self-hatred I had was already long instilled before Scott and I met. He never wanted to do anything but listen, let me know I was loved, and help me feel as much a part of our church as he could.

Scott told me now that in the years since I left he's adopted two children from China. Both of them have physical handicaps, like his own biological son whose early childhood cancer necessitated the amputation of his leg below the knee. Here again is something at which I could easily see my New York friends rolling their eyes: "Oh great, another American white Christian couple adopting foreign babies, the trendiest form of cultural imperialism! How typical. You know, the fact that they're adopting handicapped kids doesn't change the disservice they're doing them, raising them in a white-washed world where they'll never really know their own culture!" This was why I felt all warm inside when Scott mentioned, shy but proud, that his four kids speak fluent Chinese, including his two biological white children, who've been enrolled in a Chinese language school with their siblings from day one. Now that's the work of a "basic Christian dude" who's more thoughtful and nuanced than my secular sophisticates might assume.

These, I thought to myself, *were the church people who saw me and who loved me. How lucky I was.*

As I left Scott at the church office with hugs and mutual promises to stay in better touch, I headed toward the parking lot to get back in the truck. I tried all the entrances, but the church was locked. Staring at the sealed shut building, I couldn't help but think about Vincent Van Gogh's painting of "the church with no door."

Van Gogh had wanted desperately to be a pastor, but that was not in the plan as far as the Dutch Calvinist seminarians who trained him were concerned. Instead, they sent this unusual, out-of-the-box man (who some biographers believe to have been in love with his best friend, painter Paul Gaugin) as a missionary to the darkest corners of the country, refusing him a post at any of their churches.

Van Gogh's time spent among the abjectly poor miners to whom he ministered produced great art, of course (see "The Potato Eaters"), but he spent a lifetime feeling unable to find the place he longed for in the Church he loved, thus his famous "no door" painting of a beautiful but grim looking sanctuary without a way inside.

My old church is neither grim nor beautiful. The giant, purely-functional building is topped with a roof of blue corrugated steel, making it look like a steroidally overgrown IHOP. I have trouble looking at it without thinking about blintzes. And yet, standing there in front of the garish building under the hot still sun, how deeply I longed to enter it.

Suddenly another figure cut across the field toward the building. I could see it was Crossley, the oldest son of a bright and shiny, picture-perfect missionary family, who is now the middle school pastor. I waved him down and asked if he'd open the doors, and he did.

Inside, all the smells were the same—indoor/outdoor carpeting and industrial drywall. We came to the sanctuary and I went in. It was pitch dark and I couldn't see in front of me, but the chairs, still upholstered in the same cream colored carpet, hadn't changed configuration in the intervening years, so I felt my way up the center aisle until I thought to turn on my iPhone light. I shone it all around, but the glow disappeared into the cavernous worship hall, barely illuminating the stuffy silence. I made my way to the front, and leapt up onto the stage where for years I led thousands upon thousands of people in worship, performed dozens of plays, and could always look out into the crowd to see faces I knew smiling back at me. Here, again and again, I had been drawn into the presence of God with trembling, sacred joy.

Without warning my body broke, and I was overcome by grief. My chest heaved with sobs whose noise I tried to muffle, but they echoed through the space and I was embarrassed for myself, though no one was around to hear me except you. Mercifully, you didn't try to engage me or comfort me; you just let me cry. My knees bent, and I shook. No religious ecstasy here, no indwelling of the Holy Spirit, just an overwhelming sense of loss, whose sadness I have never allowed myself to feel because anger and resentment are much safer.

How could I have invested so much of myself into a place, into a community, only to wake up one day and realize I was an orphan?

Why have I gone so many years without admitting how important this world and its people were to me, and how much it hurt when I found I no longer had a home here?

I allowed myself to feel for the first time how lost I was without it, how much I missed my church.

The door opened from outside, light poured in, and it was time to go. I walked quietly across the asphalt and gravel, got in Basic Bob, and drove away.

BRAD

The Church, like any human community, is made of messed up people who will inevitably hurt others, even when trying to help.

There were some in our community who came to understand who you really were, in all your hidden isolation and self-loathing over your sexuality, and loved you anyway. Your compassionate youth pastor, who took you to breakfast, listened, encouraged you in your faith, and told you that you were loved and welcome, no matter what. And some of those high school kids actually did grow up when they got to college and beyond, welcoming you into their lives, and rejoicing in the time they spent with you, whether or not they agreed with your beliefs or moral framework. And there were those adults, most of them parents of some of your peers, who understood you earlier than you thought they did, and just kept embracing you, loving you. To this day, whenever you are in town they invite you over, take you to breakfast, watch movies with you. With them you have the freedom to be honest about who you are because they are not afraid of it, and they have the freedom to share their ideas honestly, because their acceptance of you as a person means their disagreement with you is not a threat.

Then there are those adults (who I think never really grew up) who, when they learned that you were gay, sent you scathing emails—"in love"—telling you that you would live, and mostly likely die, in misery and shame unless you turned from your "evil" ways.

These people no longer ask to see you when you are in town.

DREW

Back then, with "all systems go" for curing my secret disease, the most vexing problem with church was that it was only a few days a week. That's hardly enough treatment, if you're trying to be aggressive. *How can I experience all the healing male companionship Jesus wants for me with such inconsistent exposure to Christian community?* I wondered. What's more, by my sophomore year of high school I was beginning to get the feeling that

Church summer theater, 2004.

maybe the kind of guys who could really give me what I was lacking just weren't at my church. There seemed to be precious few boys there who had an appetite for any unbounded adventure that went beyond playing hours-long marathons of *Halo*. Or at least, the ones who did hadn't invited me on any hunting trips.

Despite my best efforts—even with help from Scott—the situation had pretty much remained "business as usual": I was popular at church and school, liked by everyone, a worship leader or a class clown, but still the phone calls I got inviting me to hang out were from girls. Though, to be fair, as my sophomore year dragged on, there was one exception.

I had made this guy friend at school, a kid from my choir and honors literature class named Omar. Even though I liked him a lot— his sly humor and intelligence becoming more evident as he let me get to know him better—Omar was . . . problematic.

First of all, Omar wasn't a Christian. His dad was a Muslim from Saudi Arabia and did something in finance, which didn't bode well if you took seriously what the Bible says about "the root of all evil." Omar's white mom wasn't a Christian either; all I knew about her was that she was really into KISS in the 80s and had seven, maybe eight, sisters. *Her* mom, Omar's Nonna, still tended bar in the outer county. At the Moose Lodge.

What's more, even though he was into theater like I was, which was cool, and had all this great knowledge about literature and philosophy, Omar was hardly an asset as far as rugged masculinity was concerned. He was more like a liability: flighty, agitated, socially awkward, driving around in his white early-90s Ford truck (the American version of the Mazda that Alex drove, incidentally), always wearing the same terrible corduroy lamb's wool coat no matter the weather, making esoteric jokes in his weird voice whose potentially masculine baritone was ruined by his idiosyncratic over-enunciation, a trait he explained as leftover from childhood speech therapy to cure a lisp but which I suspected to be psychosomatic, or even feigned altogether.

All year I'd been trying out this new urban church in Portland (in addition to our regularly scheduled family services, of course), and while I dragged Omar with me almost every weekend, he didn't really fit among the slim and artfully disheveled hipster Christians, coming across like a more delicate-featured Aladdin, if Aladdin had gotten chunky in a mid-to-late-career-Marlon-Brando kind of way. Omar's Sunday "disheveled" wasn't what you'd call artful: it had pieces of burrito stuck to it. It was nice to have him around, and the more we skipped class together to drive aimlessly in his truck the more I found I enjoyed his company, but he couldn't give me what I needed. He was a good best friend, but he didn't have the *stuff* to heal me. What I really needed was a *true immersion* experience of *total masculinity*.

I started researching Wyoming cattle ranches.

Several options were available, all of them looking for ranch hands to work and get paid through the summer, though from the looks of the pictures on the websites, I was going to need to reinvest at least half of my earnings into new denim, because nothing in my closet was remotely suitable. Remember that this was 2005, *Brokeback Mountain* hadn't come out yet, and me seeking a cure for my homosexuality on an isolated Wyoming livestock ranch was months ahead of its own irony.

Fortunately for everyone, including Wyoming, in the eleventh hour destiny intervened, and I was offered the chance to experience the rugged, male-bonded Christian community I sought so deeply, with few incurred denim expenses and even fewer cattle.

BRAD

From the time I was eight or ten years old, I went to Christian summer camps. I'll never forget the first time I went. My Dutch Mennonite, Depression-era mom told me I had to save up half the cost of the week. It cost $28. I saved my allowance for several months, did jobs, and stopped buying baseball cards. Finally I was able to give my mom a little cloth bag with twenty-eight half-dollars in it.

Fourteen bucks. My ticket to adventure.

Summer camps when I was in elementary school were just a blast of "boy craziness." Seeing if we could sneak out of our cabins at night. Locating hiding places where even a *secret agent* could not find us. In later years, middle school camp became more about checking out the girls from other church youth groups and wondering if a camp romance was in the cards that summer.

But during my high school years, instead of attending summer camps, I worked at them. From my sophomore year through much of college, I worked at a camp in the Santa Cruz Mountains of California, as a counselor, then as recreation director, and later as camp speaker. Those summers were heavenly summers.

Every day was filled, working with great people who shared my worldview, my love for God, my sense of adventure. They were summers when I was strengthened in my faith, grew in my desire to serve the Church, and felt affirmed in my culturally-typical masculinity. The outdoor kind.

No wonder then, when you talked to me about your interest in working at a summer camp, I was excited. It was soon after you mentioned this that my university had a job fair for students looking for summer work. One of the booths was from the very camp where I spent those amazing summers. *How cool it would be if Drew could spend a summer in the same camp that was so formative for me!* I thought. Perhaps a summer of working as part of a community of fun-loving young people committed to Christ would not only deepen your own faith, but also finally allow you the sense of affirmation and purpose you had sought for so long. Maybe it would even bring you the renewed strength you looked for as the happy heterosexual man we hoped you would be.

DREW

The drive down to California was filled with fearful and thrilling anticipation. You and Mom had packed my bag with all manner of mementos from home, including a six-inch stack of all our family's favorite albums, which you'd violated your conscience by burning onto CDs for me.

This would be the longest time I had ever spent away from home, but I found comfort in the music we both loved. In the absence of Mom and Dad, The Mamas and the Papas would be there. Fleetwood Mac would tell me life's hard truths (with Witchy Stevie on hand to let my dark side bloom). Clapton and Stevie Ray would make sure I never got lost, and High Priests Paul, John, George, and Ringo would be on hand to facilitate my transformation. If I got the blues—or even the Mean Reds—Eva Cassidy would sit with me in my sorrows, James Taylor would give melody to my melancholy, and when I missed you more than I could stand, all I had to do was click my heels, say, "There are no sounds like Pet Sounds," turn on anything Brian Wilson ever wrote, and smile.

I expected my mood upon arriving at the magical campgrounds full of redwoods and evergreens would be the still shot at the end of every teenage movie from the 80s, when the hero jumps into the air for a fist bump with Life and freezes in place while the credits roll over the triumphant image. I was *that* pumped. I had to be; I knew somewhere inside that this was my last shot. If this didn't work . . .

Better not to think about it.

Omar had written me a letter, which I carried with me. He didn't seem to share my faith in the nourishing intimacy with God and male peers that I so looked forward to. He told me to let go of any

Brad baptizing Drew, 1999.

unreasonable expectations I might have set for myself, which felt confusing and inexplicably enraging.

I didn't let it get me down, though.

This is going to be the best summer of my life, I thought. *It has to be.*

BRAD

To my great sorrow, the summer did not turn out for you like I had hoped. Your boss, the maintenance director, was an obsessive fanatic who found fulfillment in beds made with "hospital corners," bathroom counters scrubbed with a toothbrush, and who actually dictated how many *inches* the hangers in the cabin closets should be spaced from each other. He was working with you, a free-spirited, free-form type whose sense of proper organization was inspired by Andy Warhol. His daily disparaging evaluations of your work left you feeling worthless after only a few weeks.

But what was even worse was that your hopes for a summer full of "bonding with the guys" turned out instead to find you, weekend after weekend, alone at camp as the male staff took off on adventures without you, leaving you to hang out with the director and his little girls or doing your laundry with one of the female staff workers.

DREW

Things I Learned at Camp:

- For removing stubborn plaque or implacable self-delusion, combine one part Simple Green, two parts warm water, and one part personal inadequacy. Mix until solution appears impossible. Bubbles are normal.
- Natural Talents should be utilized only in spare hours between lonely shifts, during night skits and dramatic performances (but can include your most creative characters, i.e. mutant-hybrid Joel Grey/Liza Minelli Emcee who gives a high-kicking rendition of "Cabaret" every Friday before the weekly camp-wide talent show).

- Staff will laugh till tears at your repertoire of brilliant, blatantly queer performances, but be prepared for nine out of ten male and six out of ten female counselors to exhibit immediate discomfort in your actual presence when you're not on a stage. Awkwardness will rise commensurate to your level of no longer caring what they think.
- Kids know comedy, and will never be uncomfortable with you, even at your queerest. They will invite you to their lunch table, come to you with their problems, and tell you they wish you were their counselor. But remember, spending time with kids is "not what you're being paid to do here." For longest lasting results, mix judgment with powdered Comet; apply in a circular motion.
- Suspicions about your sexuality will be constantly hinted, but never voiced. Discomfort will manifest in proportion to how much the campers—especially the boys—think you're cool. It will eventually be implied that you might be a pedophile. Apply steel wool, scrub vigorously till hands bleed, but this particular stain rarely lifts.
- During "The Man Hike," you will hear a thirteen-year-old ask about homosexuality around the campfire; you will feel compelled to jump in, pontificating with your best ex-gay logic about "brokenness" and "SSA" and the healing potential of platonic same sex relational bonding.

As soon as the words leave your lips, you will know that you no longer believe them.

Expect that little boy's face, lit by bonfire flames and shadowed by his baseball cap, to haunt you for years.

Cover, and bring to a boil.

Chapter Six

OUT IN EGYPT

BRAD

As you continued high school, two things moved you toward deciding to live as a gay man and to turn away from Christianity—Brandon and Egypt.

You and Brandon got to know each other during rehearsals for *Hello Dolly*, your freshman high school musical. He captivated you from the start. He was smart—*brilliant*, really—funny, a talented actor, and a lot of fun. And he was from the Middle East, a huge attraction for you. You had been fascinated with the Middle East since you were a boy. Your eight-year-old birthday party, at your request, was Egyptian-themed, complete with a mummy cake and a "pin the nose on the Sphinx" game.

You both also had to deal with alienation. Brandon was attracted to men too, which, like you,

"Pin the nose on the Sphinx."

had cultural and family issues for him. As you had to deal with a sense of alienation from your faith community, Brandon, in the years after the 9/11 attacks, had to deal with the alienation experienced by many American Arabs. For him, that even meant going by a "Christian name" rather than the Middle Eastern one he is known by among his family and closest friends: *Omar*.

As your friendship with Brandon/Omar grew, your mom and I came to love him, too. Even to this day, it's always a joy when we get to be with him.

DREW

It wasn't supposed to happen the way it did.

Breaking up with Andrea after camp had felt like the only thing to do. There was no way to say what had changed in me up in the mists of the California mountains, but *something* had. I needed time to be alone.

As the days drifted from September into the long darks of December, Omar was the only friend I could be fully angry around.

St. Louis, 1997; Cairo, 2015—some things never change.

His unflappable calm kept me from despair, his deadpan zingers dispelled even my volatile self-induced crises, and the steady puttering of his foul, hoarder-level-cluttered, Mexican-food-encrusted Mazda flatbed somehow grounded me. I still dragged him to church every weekend, but I prayed for my own soul now, as well as his.

One night we had too much to drink, and without as much as "by your leave," we were having sex. He kissed me first.

Until that moment, I would have told anyone who said Omar was gay to go jump in a lake. No one ever said it though. It was never even hinted at. But suddenly, my snide Sancho had blasted away the windmills of my quixotic crusade. I felt I was in love for the first time in my life, with my best friend.

In a twist of cliché fate too stupid to be fictitious, we were cast as the buddy-leads Nathan Detroit and Sky Masterson in *Guys and Dolls* that year at our high school. We double escorted the female leads to Junior-Senior Prom.

I had spent my childhood feeling like an outcast and my youth feeling like an imposter, but with Omar I was at home in my own skin. For years he had been slowly getting to know the *real* me, my vulnerabilities and quirks and narcissistic flaws, because I'd never felt the need to put on a show for him. If Omar had been the gender-typical "bro" that I felt ex-gay ideology had me trolling for acceptance from, I would have never been able to be myself around him. But as it was, this dopey philosophe was just my day-in, day-out buddy. I learned to go to him with my sorrows and fears, knowing he'd have a better answer than anyone else, or at the very least a much funnier one. His unique perspective on life made Omar more special to me than anyone else—but in a way that snuck up on me like a riptide.

When our relationship turned physical, it felt like the answer had been in front of my face the whole time.

There was another part of me, growing smaller by the day but still fighting tooth and nail for its life, that screamed the Doom of Nations was coming if I didn't repent. This voice whispered about the frog who was placed in a pot of cold water on the stove and never noticed that the heat was being slowly turned up until it was too late and he was cooked.

You are that frog, the voice said in its trembling baritone, pointing its bony finger at me like the prophet Nathan once pointed at King David.

YOU ARE THAT FROG!

BRAD

Yes, eventually your relationship with Omar became sexual. Mom and I did not know about it until you told us. At that point all three of us were still working from the perspective that gay sex is not okay with God. You were struggling, but were still personally committed to your Christian faith. So, amazingly, you invited me into conversation with you and Omar to consider how the two of you could continue to have a close friendship without sex.

One of the major issues Robin and I had to confront was how we would handle Drew coming home with a boyfriend. Virtually all parents have to cross this bridge when their child wants to introduce them to their significant other. But for Christian parents of gay kids, the bridge can feel a bit more rickety than they'd like.

Most conservative religious parents will not think of a gay relationship in the same way as a heterosexual one, especially if they are still adjusting to their child's orientation. But if they have come to the point of accepting that their child has iden- tified as gay, they should be able not only to invite their child to bring home a same-sex significant other, but they should be able to welcome and love them, as Christians know Christ would. The one thing that might make this more conceivable is if a gay kid will commit to the same standards of behavior that parents would require of a heterosexual child. —Brad

One of the things always important to your mom and me when you kids were teenagers was for you to bring your friends over to our house. It was not that we wanted to scrutinize every person you were hanging out with. We did not have a fifty-ques- tion interrogation with a polygraph test or some more relational equivalent of that. Rather, we wanted to really know them, to let you know that we cared about your friends, and to let them know they mattered to us.

This is what happened with Omar. We knew you were attracted to each other, and that concerned us. But we also came to love him. How could we not? He was bright, funny, fasci- nating, and we could tell he valued our enjoyment. And, to be honest, we felt like the more we spent time with both of you and approved of you as persons, the more likely it would be that you would be open to our standards for dating behavior.

DREW

This was a good thing that you and Mom did. The short-term results of that strategy, looking at the hard data of how often I broke your rules of sexual behavior during this time, were mixed. However, the long-term results—me feeling valued and loved by you and Mom—were *hugely* successful. Had you been unwilling to spend time with the person who mattered to me the most, I would have always resented you for that. Instead, I look back years later with a deep appreciation for how you were willing to see the wonderful qualities of this person whom I loved—in spite of the difficulties that our homosexual relationship posed for you. This was one of the things that never allowed me to fully believe you and Mom were the monsters some of my friends would later assume you must have been.

BRAD

I'm glad. And you were so happy when you were with Omar. *Finally*, here was a boy who understood you and liked you for exactly who you were.

Of course, as much as we liked him, Mom and I were concerned. The struggle between your sexual attractions and your faith was intensifying. And, sadly for us, the acceptance and closeness you found with Omar was something you never found in the church, at least not with boys. I remember one day when we were sitting on the deck in our backyard, you talked to me about your feelings for your best friend. His companionship had filled a deep cavern of emptiness in your life which you had felt since you were a little boy. He was a male peer who knew everything about you and loved you *for who you were*.

And you loved him, too.

DREW

Throughout the months of our relationship, I went to ex-gay meet-ings and group therapy. Omar even dropped me off there plenty of times, an irony that I found excruciating but which he thought was hilarious (I only realized this years later because he was too considerate to laugh). In group, I was honest about what was going on between me and him, which elicited mostly "let's-wait-and-see" approaches from the counselors, but plenty of angry and resentful condemnation from the other group members. One guy in partic-ular was insistent that if I didn't cut Omar out of my life completely and right away, I had no business coming back to group, not when guys like him were out every night of the week shedding blood, sweat, and tears to stay on the straight and narrow.

"You think it's easy resisting temptation, huh? You think I don't get a million offers every time I go out to the bars around campus?" he said in one outburst. "I could sleep with dozens of guys tonight if I wanted to!" As I looked at his handsome blond face and thick, athletic legs, I knew he was right. "But I *don't*! And then you just come in here and flaunt your sin to all of us who are trying to get healing? You think that's helpful for us?!"

"He's trying to work this out. He wants to get better," another man cut in to my defense. "It's just that it's *complicated*. He's had a friendship with this guy for years. You want to get better, don't you Drew?" he asked, turning to me.

"I . . . I don't know what I think about it," I said. It was the first time I'd admitted this out loud. The room was silent.

"Well if you don't know what you think about it," the blond boy said, his pretty face twisted into a mask of bitterness, hot tears rolling down his cheeks, "then maybe this isn't the place for you."

That night, as I descended from the porch of the grand old house toward the darkness of the street, I saw the man who had defended me walking out to the curb. I rushed over to him, and thanked him for sticking up for me in group.

"It is complicated," I said, "and I wonder if I even know what I believe anymore. Things feel like they've been cracking for a long time. But this place has meant so much to me over the years, and I don't want to lose it. I need to keep coming here, processing what I'm going through. I really appreciate you saying something."

"No problem, Drew. I understand what it's like to—"

He was interrupted.

"Guys this is *not okay*." It was Taylor, in his firmest good-natured rebuke. He had hurried over to where we stood in the dark. "You know what our policy is about group members talking to each other outside the house. You need to go home your separate ways."

As I continued to straddle the ever-widening divide between my love for Jesus and my desire to follow him, and my love for Omar and my desire to follow Him, Omar was going through his own unheralded transformation, and it wasn't making my struggle any easier. In the course of a few months, his puppy fat melted away, like shedding a winter coat. With the help of an expensive personal trainer, he put twenty pounds back on, in hard brown muscle. His skin cleared, his thick black hair seemed to coif automatically, and he took himself shopping for the loveliest, trendiest clothes I'd ever seen in our backwater suburban town.

I never saw that lambskin corduroy jacket again in my life.

Omar's mother, who had gotten used to—and tentatively fond of—having me around the house all the time, invited me to come with the family to their apartment in New York at the end of August. I had been going through the intensive trial rounds of an application for a program that would have me visiting Egypt for June and July, a dream come true if it happened, and I figured a trip to New York would top the summer off perfectly. I'd be visiting the two places I'd fantasized about my whole life.

I pressed Omar on the details of where his father would be taking him, his sister, and his twin brother for the summer, and I finally found out they'd be spending it in Saint Tropez on his cousin's yachts. I knew his dad's extended family had access to, as Omar always put it, some "dirty oil money," but a yacht in the French Riviera sounded excessive for a boy who grew up in the Portland suburbs. Pressing him further on his heretofore enigmatic and unknowable family background, it became slowly clear that while, yes, his down-to-earth mother had been happy to raise her kids in an unassuming suburban life, Omar's dad's family, as it turned out, was kind of a big deal, as in related to a royal Persian Gulf family in ways which I cannot talk about in print, *big deal*. Omar tersely offered this as the explanation for why the young Arabs I knew at Portland State had gotten up and shook his hand in wide-eyed wonder when I introduced him by his full name.

"No one at school needs to know this please, Drew."

I wasn't the frog in the pot of boiling water; rather, I'd fallen in love with a frog, the frog kissed *me*, and before me stood a prince. Month-old-nachos-in-the-Mazda-cup holder, et al.

BRAD

During the summer between your junior and senior years, you were chosen to be one of sixteen students sent on a program funded by the US Department of State to Egypt as "junior ambassadors." We were thrilled you were chosen for this great opportunity. You would be able to visit an area of the world that had so much fascination for

"Bridging cultures," 2006.

you, learn about world politics and experience a culture quite different from your own, take Arabic classes and engage in workshops at the local universities, all while staying with an Egyptian host family in their luxurious villa. (And it didn't hurt that the US government paid for the whole thing!)

Indeed, it was an amazing summer for you. And, as traveling overseas does, it sent you back to us changed. Looking back, I think there were two things in Egypt that began to change you. You saw a different religion up close, living with and coming to love a people whose faith was very different from the one you grew up with. Also, I suspect you saw the way in which gay people were even less able to live out their identities in Egypt than they were here. I think that both saddened you and gave you a sense of resolve about your own life. When you returned, there was a distance between us that I had never felt before. You were irritable, and many of our conversations—especially about faith, which had always been enjoyable—were filled with new tension.

Something was going on.

DREW

Twice in my life God has met me, both times in the desert.

When I was ten years old, after coming from Missouri to the Pacific Northwest, we spent that first summer exploring our new home. I felt as if I'd been transported into one of my beloved adventure novels: majestic snowcapped mountains, iron seas raging against sweeping cliffs, and forests whose moss-hung trees felt as ancient and alive as the walking, talking "Ents" of J.R.R. Tolkien's Middle Earth. What a strange and wondrous land you had brought us to! Winter came, and we went on the first of what would be many family trips to "Wildhorse Canyon," in Oregon's high desert.

The rainclouds that roll in nine months of the year across Oregon are mostly empty by the time they get east of the Cascade peaks, and what stretches out toward Idaho is dry earth full of windswept plateaus above valleys of scrub brush. To one of these valleys several decades ago came the Guru Osho, the "Bagwan Shree Rajneesh," trailing eastern incense, exotic wisdom, and devoted followers who had come to live with the controversial philosopher (and his 93 Rolls Royces) in the kind of special bliss that only a sexually unhinged cult community can provide (I know this because my college apartment in New York officially fell under that category).

When the 64,000-acre ranch where the "Rajneeshees" had built their commune was disbanded amidst scandal, murder trials, and sensational global headlines, the evangelical youth organization Young Life bought it for a song, transforming the Rajneesh ghost town into a desert Christian camp paradise, complete with a 100,000-square-foot sports complex, zip line into the lake, and glistening emerald soccer fields. The lush camp nestled in the fierce high desert is a breathtaking vista, one that delighted me as we arrived for your university's annual retreat.

One morning, all us campers were sent outside to find a quiet place to pray. There was an enormous rock at the top of one of the surrounding mountains, and with the determination of a medieval pilgrim, I scaled it, then sat down in the shadow of the great stone.

As I returned to Wildhorse in following years, this "mountain" would shrink until it was revealed to have been nothing more than a hill. But the experience I had on the top never got any smaller.

I sat with my scrawny ten-year-old legs folded in a pose that even Guru Osho would have approved of, and prayed to Jesus. I had my Bible open on my lap as I stared into the dusty, billowing expanse. There was a long moment of what felt like complete silence, and then, without warning or invocation, God arrived.

God came not in the quaking earth, nor the rushing wind, nor even in a still, small voice like with Elijah in the cave. God came to me that day in a bodily experience that was visceral and real. I was rendered breathless, every hair on end, my whole body throbbing with pleasure both activating and paralyzing. The experience was of being at once shattered, filled, and totally present. The way you've described how it felt watching us kids being born sounds a lot like this. Maybe someday, against odds, I'll experience that too, and I'll let you know if it compares.

What I encountered in that moment was the presence of the Divine, and it has stayed with me forever after. What I knew in that moment was that there was a Great Force who was present in the universe, who was at that moment allowing me to enter in, to have a kind of recognition of my soul's tiny existence. Within this recognition was the fundamental knowledge—a revelation, not based in argument or proof—that I was *loved*, beyond anything I could ever do to earn such love or to lose it.

When God met me there that day, I understood Him (God was a "him" for me at the time) both as the God from the Hebrew Scriptures who I had known my whole life, yet also as a Wilder God. A Greater God. A more Unknowable and Undeniable God. This mystical knowledge of The Creator was compatible with—and at the same time somehow bigger than—all the intellectual knowledge I had about Him. Mostly, what I felt was God's overwhelming Love for His creation, and the presence of that Love in us and in everything around us.

The experience has only been repeated once, seven years later in Egypt, in the middle of the night, on the back of a threadbare nag perched above the moonlit pyramids where Cairo meets the Sahara.

A few other boys from the junior ambassador program and I had gone out for our last night of what had been a life-changing trip. My host brother knew a guy who knew a guy who would rent us horses, and soon we had set off into the dusty sand beyond the Haram gates. Having raced each other to the top of a dune, we sat, panting, in the total silence of the dark early hours. Cairo was splayed in a glittering sprawl, the great pyramids were lit up in silver by the moon in front of us, and beyond them was the eternal desert, its clean lines marred only by the far-off carcass of a camel. There were no sounds.

The first call to prayer was a solitary voice, but only for a moment. Soon it was joined by another, and another, until ten thousand minarets were bellowing the most musical and dissonant noise I'd ever heard. From our perch outside the city you could hear it all so well, this wave of interwoven Muezzin all praising God at four in the morning, calling the people of the city to come before the throne of heaven. My body reverberated, my hair stood on end, and my breath caught in my chest. The purple thickness of the vibrating air shook against my face, my pupils seemed to dilate, and as sure as I knew my name I knew I was encountering the same God I had met on that desert hill in Oregon seven years before, halfway across the world. My eyes filled with tears, and then it was over. The silence wrapped us in its heavy arms, and the air was as still as it had been before. But I was changed.

Each experience was so different. The first one felt like the beginning of that zealous fire for Christianity that consumed my youth; the second time felt like the end of it. I had been so troubled in Egypt, by so many things. My journals from Cairo display the tortured conscience of a boy terrified to lose his faith. Most of the entries end with sincere and desperate prayers. Prayers for myself, prayers for Omar, prayers to be shown something—*anything!*— that would save my crumbling belief in a God who I always thought wanted the best for me.

My journals feature the back-and-forth argument for and against the exclusive Truth of Christianity. The leather-bound pages of that diary were inscribed "backwards," from right to left, (in an effort to get me to practice my Arabic). The farther along you go, the more desperate the entries become, appealing to Christ. *Be with me here, Jesus. Come, Jesus—meet me here. Jesus come. Jesus.*

Eventually the entries just stop.

Once I'd met God for the second time, not at a Christian camp in Oregon but in a Muslim call to morning prayer, my mindset changed. What I had grown up believing to be a matter of measurement and truth became one of perspective and interpretation. These people over here were just like the ones I knew at home, and suddenly I realized that I no longer believed they were going to hell.

Something shifted inside me that has never really shifted back.

By the time I came home to Portland, life had fallen apart. A week spent in Omar's Manhattan apartment had been torturous. Omar's father had become aware of the nature of our relationship, and the tension in the luxurious but cramped downtown flat was thicker than his Gulf accent. Omar had been inexplicably cold and unresponsive, sending me into a tailspin of frantic emotional neediness and codependent panic. A year older than me and now graduated, he would be staying in New York for school in September, while I would return alone to our suburban town. Omar stopped talking to me as soon as I left the city, and it would be over a year before I learned that his father's knowledge of our relationship had been made clear to Omar in Europe that summer (though not before he'd racked up a $2,000 trans-Mediterranean phone bill calling me in my Cairo tour bus from his cousins' Ferraris in Monaco). For the next eighteen months, I would go on living under the assumption that Omar had abandoned me without any intention to come back. As far as I knew, I was alone.

At home, one clear September day while walking through our neighborhood by myself, I looked up at the beautiful blue sky above the mountains.

I will lift up mine eyes unto the hills, from whence cometh my help.

I felt, for the first time in my life, hatred and brokenhearted fury at God, the friend who had walked with me in every lonely moment from the time I was first aware that I didn't belong where I was supposed to.

Some help you've been all these years. I've done everything you've asked. I've given you all that I have, and it hasn't been enough. I kept myself as pure as I could, searched for the healing of my brokenness through your Church and everywhere I was supposed to, and still you let me fall in love—which I never wanted!—and now he's gone and I'm unable to pretend that I don't know what I've lost, or that I wouldn't give anything to have it back, even if that condemned me to hell forever. THIS is hell. This has been hell, all along. I'm done feeling pain now. I'm done feeling shame and fear of being found out. It's over between You and me.

I shouted now.

"F*** you. You're not worth it."

BRAD

You had always told your mom and me about virtually all the things going on in your life, even when you knew they would be an issue with us. But in your senior year, you cut way back on how much you shared.

Clearly things were going on that we did not know about. And you weren't talking.

You decided to leave the worship team at church, telling us that in good conscience you didn't feel like you could sing some of the things you were singing. Finally, during the middle of your senior year, you came to Mom and me one weekend and told us you did not want to go to church anymore. That you no longer believed.

It was a devastating moment for me.

When I was five years old, I went to a summer Bible club for a week. My earliest memories of hearing about God's forgiveness of my sin and His deep love for me in Christ come from that week. That was when I first believed in Jesus as the forgiver of my sin. Later, my freshman year in high school, I went to a weekly Bible study with our new youth pastor. Through his teaching, the story of the Bible came alive to me. In that ancient story I sensed the love of God, heard Him calling me to follow Him with my life. I believed that God had seen me in my sin, had reached out to me in love through Christ—that He had saved me by drawing me into relationship with Him.

As a result of that encounter, I came to believe that connecting with God, finding true hope in this life and for a life beyond this earthly one, somehow had to go through Jesus Christ. I had gone to college and seminary and done a PhD in theology all as part of a commitment to understand this story and to share it with people and help them understand it, to live it out. That included my children.

The day you told Mom and me you were leaving the church, I thought back to the famous passage in Deuteronomy 6 where Moses tells the fathers of Israel to learn the story of God's salvation well, to "bind it upon your foreheads and your wrists," to "write it on the tablets of your hearts," to tell it to their children so that they too would come to faith in the God of the Bible.

In that moment, when you told me you were leaving the church, that you did not believe anymore, not only did I have deep concern for your life, I also felt like a failure as a father. *Somehow,* I thought, *I've failed to live out the story of Christ in a way that drew you to embrace it, to hold onto it.*

Not everyone's LGBTQ story leads them to reject their faith. But when I was seventeen, my new understanding of my sexuality shook the very foundation of my belief. If that is the case, it might be better for a queer or questioning kid not to reveal all that to their parents immediately.

I did reveal all that to my poor parents at once and I wish I hadn't, for both our sakes. I was seventeen. I was still so far from knowing who I was going to be at thirty, or which of the things I had grown up with I would take into adulthood or leave behind. In dumping my entire crisis of sexual identity and faith on my parents in the dramatic way that I did, I alienated myself from them—especially from my dad, whose whole life revolves around his faith—in a way that didn't really serve any of us.

I think what's needed to ease this conversation over the years is living out one of the most beautiful passages of the Bible:

Paul's famous fruit of the Spirit: love, joy, peace, patience, kindness, goodness, faithfulness, gentleness, and self-control. It's amazing how far these go to change a conversation.
—Drew

The rest of that year and the following summer were hard times for our relationship. There was distance and an anger bubbling just below the surface—except when it frothed over and exploded. Our relationship suffered that year as much because of my own feelings of failure as it did because of your need to distance yourself from me. I am sorry about that. I was angry at you for rejecting the truth that I felt I had so clearly and rationally explained to you on so many occasions through the years. Surely, I felt, any thinking person would be convinced by my arguments for the faith. Why weren't you?!

In rejecting the faith, you were rejecting *me*.

At least that's how I felt.

My parents are good people. I'm lucky. But things weren't always like they are now. When I was coming out at home, my dad and I fought all the time. There were moments when I said unfair and hateful things, and moments when my dad raged, pressing his arguments beyond all reason. It got so bad that I moved out.

Years later, I realized that the more grace and respect I could show my parents, the more I could respect myself. If I spoke with kindness and compassion in spite of my (sometimes justified) anger, if I listened to them and tried to hear their point of view, if I tried to consider their feelings as well as my own,

> *I felt good at the end of the argument, no matter how it turned out. I wish both of us had learned this earlier.*
>
> *The situation with my parents taught me the value of seeking a working relationship with those closest to us, rather than always seeking to win arguments or alter others' core beliefs.* —Drew

One Saturday afternoon, everyone was out of town except for us. I had been feeling an increase in disrespect from you for Mom and me—disregarding our house rules and exhibiting a growing sense of disdain for our role as parents. We had a really heated argument, an argument that spilled out of the house and onto our driveway. I pushed you, a moment I will always regret. "That's it," you said. "I'm leaving."

And you did.

You crammed a tangle of clothes into a backpack along with your toothbrush, stormed out of the house, and didn't come back for months.

I was devastated. *How could this be happening?* Worse, Mom and the other kids were away for the weekend, so I had to spend the rest of it by myself with gnawing agony in my gut, wondering if my relationship with you was over. It was awful. But then Mom came home, helped me climb out of the pit of despair, and we realized that this could be a good thing.

When you left that day, you did not go live under a bridge or hop a freight train to locations unknown and sever all communication with us. Thank God! Instead, you called a friend and asked if you could crash there for a few days. A few days turned into the rest of your senior year. This friends' parents, though we did not know them well, were evangelical Christians, and they became a godsend.

At first, it was very difficult for Robin and me that Drew would leave to live with another family. We felt like failures for a couple weeks. As evangelicals, sometimes we feel pressure to have life totally together, to build perfect Christian families. Of course the reality is that we are all far from that, but sometimes we're ashamed to admit it.

But once we moved beyond these feelings of failure, we found that Drew's time away from home actually gave us the opportunity to grow in ways we couldn't have while living in the same house. Drew had the relief of not feeling like we were always looking over his shoulder. This allowed our interactions to be much more civil and enjoyable.

Drew also did something on his own that was kind and helpful to us. He occasionally invited us over on a Friday night to join him, his friend, and their family to play games. I would rather watch paint dry than play most board games, but just the experience of being invited to spend time with him in an environment where we all had to be civil was healing.

Ironically, the rules that Drew's new family laid out for him were more restrictive than ours. (Wow, did he have to do a lot of yard work!) But they were made by people who were not interested in addressing the morality of his life, so he had no problem abiding by them.

After several months, we made a new start. He moved back in with us and stayed until he left for New York. Those months were not without conflict, but the time apart helped us go back to the place of seeing that we fundamentally loved and appreciated each other, and that reality mattered more than the things we were fighting about.

When negotiations break down, sometimes it's best to take a break. In our case, that meant residential relocation. On more

Your moving out made me feel like a failure. But in the big picture, it was what we needed. Those months gave us the necessary space to communicate with less anger and to begin to negotiate a new stage in our relationship. The two major factors of that altered relationship were that you would no longer be a Christian, and that you were going to openly embrace your gay identity and live a gay lifestyle.

This was a difficult reality for Mom and me, but we had been preparing for it for a long time. We felt sad but not shocked. If this was the direction that you chose to go, we would continue to love you and accept you as our son, no matter what.

While accepting an LGBTQ kid even if disagreeing with their lifestyle may seem like what any loving parent would do, it is not always the case in the Christian community or among other conservative branches of faith. Many parents either remain in some kind of denial of the fact that they have a gay son or daughter, or they reject them.

Our love for Drew as well as our biblical convictions made both of those approaches unacceptable. We believe in a God who never turns away from those He loves, even when we turn from Him. We knew that the most important factor in continuing to have a voice in our son's life was to stay as positive in our relationship with him as possible. God's love for us in Christ had shown us that if you are going to love someone, you love them unconditionally.

But for us to have personal integrity, that love did not mean we would be okay with anything Drew did, especially if he was going to live in our house with our support. We knew that Drew, like all our kids, would have to make his own adult decision about continuing in the faith we'd chosen. As much as we hoped and prayed he would remain in that faith, it had to be honest. If he could no longer hold that faith honestly, then integrity demanded he move on. We would not make any faith demands on him. But we would have to figure out what that meant practically for our family. —Brad

On the issue of a sexually active gay lifestyle, though, we had to deal with things a bit differently. Mom and I had moral convictions about gay sex that we had to be honest about. We felt that since we were still providing a home for you and providing your basic needs, we had the right to construct some family agreements about how you would respect our home space. We decided to address it in exactly the same way we would address a sexual situation with a heterosexual son or daughter. It was not okay, according to those rules, say, for your younger sister to have a sexual relationship with a boyfriend in our house. For us, home rules about sex were not simply a homosexual issue. So we told you that we were not okay with you having sex under our roof. On the other hand, we told you we would welcome any friend you brought into our home: male or female, gay or straight.

Thinking about "negotiations" with a son or daughter feels strange. After all, what parent, remembering first holding their child, thought they'd be using a word that belongs in sentences with "cease-fire" and "corporate take-over" to describe communicating with their precious child? But there come moments in navigating the relationship with your LGBTQ child when you realize you are negotiating a truce, or the terms of a mutual compromise. That's just the way things are—love and real relationship can still happen in the middle of the "negotiations."

At this point, religious parents have accepted that their main job is not to figure out or "fix" their gay kid—and the child has accepted that their parents' beliefs are probably not going to change. Rather than both parties trying to convert each other, the goal becomes figuring out how to live together.

I've learned that the starting place is mutual respect. This is not a mutuality of peers; parents have a rightful place of authority over their growing minor children. Kids need to respect their parents, understanding that being provided for means accommodating some of their own behavioral choices to their parents' guidelines. But parents need to respect their gay children by creating ground rules in the home to deal with behavior rather than attractions or personal expression—the same rules they would insist upon for a heterosexual child.

Deciding what constitutes these ground rules will be tricky at first. A whole array of realities may accompany the fact that a child identifies as gay. Parents need to carefully consider which they are willing to live with and which they aren't. Then they need to patiently negotiate with their child as issues come up. In short, choose your battles.

A lot depends on the age of the child; parents rightly have more restrictions on a child who is thirteen than on one who is seventeen. And once the child is of age, negotiations for household behavior change to negotiations between adults. —Brad

As followers of Christ, your mom and I are called to love our neighbors, no matter who they are. To this day, we have loved the gay friends you have brought into our lives and have never regretted that for a moment.

Drew, I just want to say that at that point, your mom and I decided that we would make our relationship with you the primary life issue for us. If you walked away from the Christian faith, we would be sad, but we would accept your decision. If you decided to live a life in harmony with your same-sex attractions, it would be a struggle for us, but we would accept you, *fully*.

You are our son. The moment I first saw your face I knew I would lay down my life for you. Nothing has ever changed that and nothing ever will. We have made mistakes, traded hurts. But never has my father's love faltered toward you, Son. As I have told you many times, you are a gift to me from God. I am so thankful to Him for giving *you* to us. Because of you I am a better dad, a better person, and even a better Christian.

Kids, people you love are probably going to say some ignorant things, perhaps things like, "Why would you choose this?" or "Why would you do this to us?" or "The idea of you being that way makes me sick to my stomach" or "Aren't you afraid of AIDS?" Especially if they're coming from your parents, these things may hurt you or make you angry. That's okay! But also have patience with them. Like you may have been for a long time, they're frightened and unsure of how to move forward. As weird as it may feel, you may have to hold your parents' hand through the process, especially at the beginning. You may have to create a space of peace and calm inside your own heart to which you can return, over and

Once you decided to leave the church, our walks together became much less frequent. When we did walk together, it felt to me like we were two porcupines who deeply wanted to hug each other but *couldn't*. I think the frequency of my evening walks actually increased, but it was usually just me and the dog. For him, these strolls were just as magical as ever, and while I'm sure his canine intuition told him that something was wrong, his looks said, *Come on, Dad, isn't it enough that we're together? Isn't this fun?* Labrador Retrievers are just that way.

My walks were filled with prayer, much more so now that God was the only person to talk to. But life had changed, and the question now was, *What do I pray for?* Before, my prayers for you had gone something like, "Dear God, please give Drew the strength to trust you in the midst of his same-sex attractions so that he can resist the temptation to live a gay life." That prayer seemed irrelevant now. For a very brief time, my prayers went something like, *God, you are all powerful and loving. You can make Drew straight. Please do.* But that prayer was short-lived. I had been teaching the Bible long enough to know that God's normal reaction to human struggle is not to take it away, but to give people the grace to endure. Moreover, I knew too many stories of gay Christians who prayed for years that God would make them straight. I don't know a single person for whom that prayer worked, at least the way they wanted it to work.

So I stopped praying that God would make you straight. I stopped praying that you would not have gay sex. I didn't even pray that you would have sex with a woman and find it surprisingly more fulfilling.

I also didn't pray that God would make you miserable. But some of our friends did.

Once, when Mom was visiting some friends from college and telling your story, one of them told her, "I am going to pray that Drew will be so disgusted with his life that he will repent of his sin and turn back to Christ." I get the sentiment of that prayer, kind of like, "What's a little suffering if it turns someone back to God?" Mom, too stunned to respond at the time, eventually told me what she wished she had said: "Oh please *don't do that*. Drew already experiences more shame and self-loathing than you can imagine. More of that will not save him, but it may kill him."

No, my prayer for you began to take on a whole new character. I stopped praying about your homosexuality and started praying about something much more important. I began to pray that God would be gracious to allow you to be so captivated by Christ's love for you, that you would want Jesus more than anything else. And if that began to happen, I would let God worry about the rest.

Drew recently met a woman from a local Christian university who volunteers several days a week with different homeless outreach centers and youth shelters, some church affiliated, some not. Every single day she encounters young people who *live on the streets because their Christian parents sent them packing as soon as they discovered they were queer. The numbers are overwhelming.*

This often happens because of a sense of religious faithfulness or integrity. Many parents feel like they are standing up for their Christian convictions. They may also feel like this is the most effective and, perhaps, even the most "loving" way to save their child from ungodly behavior that could lead to destruction and perhaps final judgment by God.

But Robin and I recognized that whatever influence we wanted to have in Drew's life would come by staying in relationship. We knew that to disconnect from him relationally would be devastating to Drew, and not in the sense that some suggested to us—that perhaps he would hit bottom, see the error of his ways, and repent—but that he would hit bottom and probably never come up.

I recently read a story (I have read too many of these) about the death of a boy kicked out of his home for being gay. His Christian mother told him to get out of the house and only come back when he "stopped being gay." Desperate and without enough money to survive, he tried calling her to talk out their differences, but she would not answer. The next time she saw him he was in a casket, dead from a drug overdose. If you do kick your gay adolescent kid out of the house, the chances they will end up physically and sexually abused or addicted to drugs and/or alcohol increase dramatically. Adolescents—gay or straight—who are separated from their families, especially for reasons of relational alienation from parents, are far more likely to end up in serious trouble than those who live at home.

I don't say that to scare or shock. But the realities here can be life and death. Relational disconnection always leads to destruction. —Brad

As a whole family, we had never had a discussion about your sexuality. Before you moved to New York, you wanted to talk face-to-face with Breegan and Corey, your sister and brother, so they could hear who you were from your own mouth rather than simply having to respond to rumors at church and school. You wanted them to be able to ask you questions if they had them. Breegan was sixteen at this time and already knew anyway. But your brother was only twelve and did not have the same level of awareness.

So we went to a house on the Olympic peninsula in Washington for a weekend. It was just across the street from the beach. Especially in the winter, this is not a hot and sunny southern California beach, but a section of coastline pummeled by rain and wind. I have always loved the beach in that kind of weather. The water churned by the storms and the wind against my face has always spoken to me about the fact that life is full of challenges and often with painful struggles. Yet I cannot witness the ocean's majesty, even when it is angry, without sensing that somehow God is present, assuring me I am safe in His love even when life is confusing.

From the sister . . .

My big brother was my hero growing up. He and I invented hundreds of our own worlds. Dreaming up a new adventure every day, we were the king and queen of our childhood. Drew took the lead in most of the imagining, and I followed him willingly, captivated by his spirit. He dressed me until I was sixteen (even after Drew moved to New York, I'd call him in the mornings to consult about my wardrobe, until finally he announced I had graduated from fashion apprenticeship and could dress on my own). To me, Drew could do no wrong. I was his loyal defender, his willing accomplice, and his unwilling model for new hairstyles. He was my best friend.

But on a late summer day when I was fifteen, I found out. He told me all about his "involvement" with Omar, that yes, he was gay, and he wouldn't (couldn't) change. I didn't understand—he had dated girls in the past. I had just told someone off for calling him a faggot (I promise, I was wholly unaware and this conversation came as a huge surprise, despite millions of hints). But . . . doesn't Drew love Jesus? Doesn't he know the Bible better than me?

Suddenly those evening counseling sessions years ago at Dr. Adams's office made much more sense. (I never understood why I hadn't been invited to therapy with Drew, Mom, and Dad. Corey and I waited in the lobby, played on the Sit 'n Spin, and watched Space Jam. Great sibling bonding, but I still felt left out and sensed secrets.)

I'm ashamed at some of the thoughts I had the moment Drew told me he was gay. I felt shock, fear, and disbelief. I'm sorry to say that up until that moment I believed many of the lies I had heard about gay people (the pervading sense that they were "special sinners"). But everything changed when I realized two things.

One: the boy looking back at me was my brother. My dear friend. My favorite person. He wasn't any more or less human or worthy of love and belonging because of this part of him.

Two: based on my understanding of the Bible, if Jesus were here today, he would not be hanging out with me (because I fit into the culture of Wednesday night youth groups and Sunday morning worship). No, if Jesus were physically present now, *he would be with Drew. He spent his time with the marginalized, the people whom the religious labeled "unfit." Who are we to say who is welcome in our community when Jesus spent his life loving the people who were cast out of society?*

Deciding whether living an LGBTQ lifestyle is right or wrong is not on my agenda. I have better things to do than skirmish over this one issue (there are hungry and sick people in the world; I'd rather talk about how to fix those problems). My

Sibling times in Times Square, 2010.

opinion on this issue is shaped and reshaped both by people I know and love and the scriptures I study to know and experience God. Sure, I may have an opinion, but as a Christian, my call to love people trumps everything else. My job is to love whole people as a whole person. To listen to the stories of people who have been marginalized, and respond with the kindness, love, and acceptance I know Jesus would.

I cannot say, "I know how you feel," but I can say, "Here is love." —Breegan Harper

It was a great weekend. The conversation you had with your siblings was profound, incredibly affirming of our family's closeness. By the time of that getaway your sister already knew and just wanted to affirm you. Your brother had been so young during most of this journey, that we had decided not to talk to him much about something we figured he would have a hard time understanding. It was all a bit new for your brother, but he knew that something was going on. As it turned out, most of what he had heard had been rumors from friends at school who had older siblings who knew you. They had teased him about you being gay and he had become very defensive.

It was powerful to hear your brother and sister tell you that whoever you are, you are their brother, they love you, and they weren't about to let people get away with "dissing" you.

Mom and I did not really have to say much. The relationship between the three of you guided the conversation.

And it was beautiful.

Chapter Seven

IN OLD
NEW YORK

BRAD

After a summer of selling kitchen knives (very successfully, I might add), you made the decision to go to New York City. After graduating high school, you had been accepted at Tisch School of the Arts, a prestigious conservatory for theater at New York University. But even with scholarships, we simply could not afford to send you. For a while you thought you would just go to public university in Washington, but then you decided—like so many hopeful actors, artists, and musicians of ages past—that you would head off to NYC and see what happened.

What no one could have anticipated was what would happen before you left. A call came into your high school front desk from a woman we'd never heard of, but who would change your life.

DREW

"Good morning, Mountain View High School, how may I direct your call?"

"Is this where Drew Harper goes to school?"

"Yes . . . Dear God, what has he done now?"

"Ahem. My name is Patti Andersen Leigh, and I'd like to be Drew Harper's fairy godmother, and make all his dreams come true. Now would you please give me his parents' phone number? Thank you."

While the no-nonsense surrealism of this dialogue may sound straight out of a Wes Anderson movie, it was in fact the word-for-word transcript of the call that came in the last week of my senior year. There was no precursor to this woman's inquiry, save an article written about me in the local newspaper a month before.

Splashed across the front page of the Living section of our native suburban rag—complete with full color photographs and interviews with you and Mom and my high school music teacher—this article told the story of a local youngster, star of his high school's yearly musical, who had been accepted to NYU's theater program. Unable to afford it on the decidedly middle class income of his two teacher parents, this plucky kid had summoned every ounce of good ol' American moxie he had and decided to head for the Big Apple with only the clothes on his back and the dreams in his heart. (*Cue Liza Minelli* New York, New York! *soundtrack with traveling montage ending in Times Square.*)

The article, a human interest piece, had indeed caught the interest of one particular human, sitting across town on her massive riverside veranda with a Bloody Mary and her daily Sudoku puzzle. The punchy opener was what grabbed her: "At five years old, Drew Harper told his parents he needed an agent."

She had been unable to get this funny little five-year-old out of her mind and vacillated for a month before finally deciding to call the local high school and tell them exactly what was going to happen. Next, she'd tell the parents.

Then, at last, the boy would need to be informed, of course.

On the Sunday afternoon when Patricia Andersen Leigh arrived in our driveway, her siren red Lexus SC convertible looking wildly out of place at the end of our sleepy middle-class cul-de-sac, she was wearing the *best* outfit. Crisp white culottes with golden links at the calf, a canary yellow sweater set, and the cutest white and gold sandals you ever did see. Two diamonds large enough to alleviate Argentina's national debt sparkled on her ring finger and in a simple pendant around her soon-to-be-lifted-and-tucked neck—"Nothing drastic, darling. No Beverly Hills stretch job or anything like that. It's just that at seventy-five years old you have to trim your edges. Like wiping the condensation off your chardonnay."

I wasn't living with you and Mom at the time; I was still in my friend's basement across town. Things between us had been awful, often exploding, and there was little warmth between you and me. In the journal entry for that date—July 1, 2007—I note my annoyance that faking the 'Happy Harper Family Show' would be necessary. My mind was occupied by other considerations, such as how many CUTCO kitchen knife order forms I still needed to fill out, and whether the proceeds from the sales would be enough to cover my estimated costs for New York rent.

> When you're newly out, it can be infuriating to interact with your religious parents. It's maddening to hear them telling you the way you fall in love is dirty and wrong and shameful.

Even if those aren't their words, that's exactly how it feels. I can remember having difficult conversations like this many times during that first year. So how do you talk about such an issue, loaded as it can be with feelings that make you want to scream at them or just turn your back?

The answer is patience. It takes time, and the decision—which is a living decision, one you have to keep making over and over—to listen to your parents express their beliefs and continue to seek a meaningful relationship together.

Looking back, my process of communicating this to Mom and Dad was halting and half-baked. I waited until the pent-up frustration exploded at the most inopportune moments. I wish someone had told me what I'm telling you: be patient, be kind. Once you have given them the opportunity to express what they think, you must tell them, graciously but firmly, that they're going to need to move on. —Drew

I had been informed that a woman named Leigh—presumably of the massive chain of Leigh luxury auto dealers stretching from Colorado to Seattle to southern California—had called the school after reading that article. She'd sent me an elegant graduation note, saying she would meet me soon. This intrusion necessitated I come back to your and Mom's house—the last place on earth I wanted to be—paste on a smile, pretend our relationship hadn't fallen to pieces, and talk to this person I'd never met about . . . *what,* exactly?

Patti Leigh is coming over this afternoon, my journal reads, *and I have no idea what I'll do or say.* This was the last thing I would write in this journal for almost two years.

As I opened the door, Patti's laugh-lined face split into a

megawatt smile. One of her ring fingers was in a splint, but the wrapping tape matched her outfit, something I somehow discerned to have been premeditated.

> *Whatever you do, don't simply stop talking about the issues. But make sure that your conversations with your child about their sexuality are not about your anger or shame. If they are, then your child will quickly recognize the conflict is really about you and not them. You owe it to yourself, to your child, and to God to express clearly and honestly your disagreement with your child's decision to live out a non-heterosexual sexuality, but then you have to move beyond that. If your child decides to move in a different direction, then the conversation needs to be about how to stay in loving relationship in spite of serious disagreement. This is not the same as just agreeing to disagree and then living the rest of your lives with a rainbow elephant in the room. Not talking about it can be as relationally damaging as waging verbal warfare. —Brad*

Over a home-cooked Sunday brunch, Patti Leigh informed you, Mom, and all three of us children that she had "made a decision." She'd read the article. She thought I sounded like a very promising and ambitious young man. Her late husband Donny, scion of the luxury auto empire, had died a little over a year ago, leaving her very well taken care of financially but very lonely and, to be frank, *bored*. Donny had been her adventure partner. They'd spent their life together jet setting across the world, first as trysting lovers, then as man and wife, and always looking for the most fun there was to be had. Upon his death, she'd found that the hobbies of those in her age group and socioeconomic class—golf, pinochle, and discussing Republican politics—could hardly keep her amused very long. She desperately needed, she told us, "a project." After reading the article, she had decided this project ought to be the financing of this precocious five-year-old's university education. Now what did we say to that?

What, indeed, *does* one say to something like that?

Once the silence had been broken by the sound of us dusting off our jaws as we rolled them slowly back into our heads, Mom finally said, "Well, Patti. That's a very generous offer. We'll have to take some time to talk about it, as a family. Would you like any dessert?"

"No thank you," Patti smiled—but she wouldn't say no to a Stoli on the rocks with a twist if we had it.

Unfortunately, we were *fresh* out.

The summer proceeded quickly after that. Several days a week, after finishing my morning shift at the local bakery, I headed to Patti's sprawling penthouse condo on the Columbia River, where the two of us grand old dames got to know one another. Patti told me tale after tale of her wild and unusual life, stories I imbibed with even more gusto than the liquor she patiently taught me how to mix, serve, and drink, and I kept her laughing with stories of my own. While the deadline to enroll in NYU that September had passed, Patti said it would be no problem for me to start the following year, after spending the interim in New York getting my urban sea legs. She would visit me often, she told me. New York, as she knew well, could be so much *fun*.

"You don't think it'll be a problem to get back into NYU, do you?" she asked one night,

"Not at all," I replied. "Patti, I really can't believe what you're doing for me. It's not something I ever could have imagined. I'm going to work so hard to deserve it, I promise."

"My Darling Boy," she smiled, "you must call me *Gramma*."

BRAD

When I think today of Gramma Patti and her involvement in your life, I break out in a smile. Patti is one of a kind, for sure. She is fun, fashionable, adventurous, and moves through life with a spirit much younger than her years. To some people, it may seem odd for a man in his mid-twenties to be so relationally connected to a woman who is now an octogenarian and whom he had never met until he was eighteen years old. But you have always had relationships with amazing women the age of your parents, or even older, so for you to be visiting museums, traveling, and going to shows with a woman like Patti was not out of our comfort zone by the time she came into your life.

Patti arrived when your relationship with me was in a crisis over the disagreements around the way you wanted to live your life. When you left home with Patti's offer to help you go to a university we could not afford, your mom and I also knew that it was providing you with the opportunity to immerse yourself in the world of New York City. While amazed at her unprecedented and generous offer, I knew it meant that a whole universe of possibility would be open to you—full of both good things and things that scared me.

As rough as the last year had been for us, I was not looking forward to you leaving. For eighteen years we had laughed together, argued together, read together, sung together, talked philosophy and theology and history together. What other father and son kill time on a road trip by naming Civil War generals? Like any parent about to send their son away to school, I knew that when you left, there would be a huge hole in my life. And you would be so far away.

As a follower of Christ and as a parent who wanted to see my son live out the faith I had taught him, for several years of Drew's adolescence I only focused on my hope that Drew would make the celibate/heterosexual marriage decision. Perhaps his relationship with Andrea pushed those hopes even higher. So when Drew finally told us he was leaving the church, abandoning his faith, and had decided to live as a gay man, his decision hit me like a ton of bricks. It took months for me to begin to dig out from under the pile of my anger and guilt, and for a while I simply did not know how to relate to him.

I wish I had been better prepared. One part of doing that is to anticipate what you will do if your son or daughter doesn't become the stereotypical "victory over sin" story. —**Brad**

I knew I would rarely see you (for who knows how long?), but I was also afraid. New York, for all its opportunities, is also a city that chews people up and spits them out with impunity. You were strong, smart, and on a mission. But you were also vulnerable. My father's heart feared for you.

Family photo the night Drew left for New York City, 2007.

To top it all off, just before you left, our precious Labrador retriever, Chip, had to be put down. That was *horrible*. I'll never forget him walking down the hallway with the vet, wagging his tail and turning around. He looked at me as if to say, "Aren't you coming, Dad?" We all stood in the parking lot and wept. So I wasn't in great shape emotionally when Mom and I took you to the airport to put you on a red-eye flight to New York.

It was National Coming Out Day the morning you arrived in New York. I was clueless about the irony, but your mom was very aware of it. There would be no one meeting you at the airport. You would have to make your own way. You slept in the train station your first night. Eventually you found more permanent lodging—an illegal sublet. The windows were covered with newspaper by the paranoid nutcase who rented it to you. Finally, by the beginning of the next year, you had two jobs, a great roommate, and a better place to live. That spring you auditioned for Tisch once again, and were accepted. "Gramma" Patti was determined to take care of your college tuition.

But within a year or so, Patti's support moved from being only about college tuition to bankrolling a whole *lifestyle*, including a swanky townhouse, a credit card, and a spending allowance. Mom and I felt this would not end up serving your best interests. But you were already thousands of miles away from us, on your own journey—one that you were determined to see through.

So we waited.

DREW

It's one thing for a suburban "post-Christian" gay boy to go to New York and experience the city's plethora of characters and world-views; it's quite another thing for that boy to be skyrocketed into the circles of Manhattan's über-elite, without any previous preparation for such a change. I was from small town evangelical America, and the wild world I came to inhabit in New York meant class-culture-shock of epic proportions.

I was surrounded by secular, privileged New York kids—kids who took the material lifestyles I had always pined for completely for granted. It had a profound effect on my attitude toward the religious, middle-class upbringing I came from: *If these people who have the lives I've always wanted exhibit such contempt and confusion toward my parents' faith, I guess the world I came from is something to be ashamed of.* I felt a panicked urge to distance myself from my former world, my former self. That included you.

The role Patti played in my life was not only a fun-seeking adventure partner, but a surrogate parent. She was delighted I was gay, and more than willing to enter into the gay New York universe as a benevolent, gay-supportive "parental unit." Not only could she do this without any internal religious conflict, she could also do it with an unlimited line of credit, something she increasingly

delighted in making available to me in her quest to make me into the ambitious, cosmopolitan son she'd never had and always wanted.

It became very easy to feel smug and self-satisfied when

comparing myself to you, Mom, and the home I left behind. Gramma Patti's largesse, combined with her secularist celebration of my gay identity, had the unintended consequence (one of several) of enhancing my anti-religious bitterness, extravagantly highlighting everything I had "missed out on" during my years of faithfully serving God and humbly submitting my sexuality to Him for healing.

"Wow," I thought to myself, "Patti is the parent I *should* have had, and certainly this is the social class I *should* have been born into. Thank God I finally arrived where I belong!"

BRAD

I honestly did not worry much about Patti "replacing" me and your mom. Most young people, especially those moving away from their parents' influence or struggling with their wishes, find themselves meeting other "parental figures" who see the world more like they do. Many of them wonder why they couldn't have been born to these parents instead. I knew you would work through that.

I was sure you were convinced, no matter how much we butted heads about your life, that I *loved* you.

But this is something most evangelical parents of gay kids will have to deal with. Some of their kids' friends, both peers and parental figures, will be horrified by parents who can't fully affirm their children's sexuality. Some will portray such parents as monsters, people whose influence is destructive and should be avoided at all costs.

But for a parent to try and separate their gay kid from those people—which will always fail and likely drive the beloved kid even further away—is not the choice your mom and I made. We decided just to welcome these people, including Patti, into our lives. They would see we were not monsters, and we believed our acceptance of them would make it more likely that you would stay close to us.

> When some people meet a gay person, they have a difficult time thinking about them through any other lens other than that they are gay. Over the years I have heard some Christians talk about a celebrity or an artist with great appreciation . . . until someone pipes up, "Yeah, but you know he's gay, right?" As if that somehow negated their admirable qualities or contributions.
>
> For many evangelical parents of a gay son or daughter, their child's sexuality becomes so overwhelming that they have difficulty thinking of them in any other terms. This can skew our ability to see the wonderful qualities of our kids. Instead, we need to move our child's sexuality to the back burner of the relationship, choosing to focus on them as whole people, and keep doing the things we have always loved doing together. —Brad

I think Patti was wise enough to see how genuine our love for you was, which is why she never portrayed us to you as harmful or clueless, no matter what you might have been feeling. As it worked out, Patti simply became a loved and cherished part of our family. We are all *so* glad she entered our lives through you. When I think of Patti's singular involvement in your extravagant New York experience, her enthusiasm for your gay identity was truly not a main concern for me—I knew that if you were going to be part of the gay subculture, you were going to do it with abandon and drama whether or not you did it with Patti's budget. Honestly, my main concern was that the money she lavished on you would result in you becoming dependent upon her rather than on your own hard work.

And that's what happened.

DREW

By the summer of 2009, there really were no rules anymore.

In July I arrived home from Paris, where I had spent the summer skateboarding around the Left Bank, shopping at Chanel, and licking gourmet gelato at Le Jardins du Rodin by day, then pretending to understand French techno music by night. Gramma Patti had developed Achilles tendonitis right before the trip, but that wasn't enough to stop us from having fun—not the two of us queens!

Each afternoon I loaded her into a wheelchair, rolled her to the bridge outside our rented flat, and crossed the Seine to the Louvre for our daily picnic lunch in the imperial palace gardens, Le Tuileries. Piled on Gramma's lap each day was a great woolen blanket folded into quarters; our wicker picnic basket full of fresh breads, cured meats, cheeses, a chardonnay bottle for her and a Sancerre bottle for me; and finally, perched on top, the vintage Bennett-Vector trucks of my favorite periwinkle skateboard framed her laughing blue eyes.

From this magical summer I came back to Manhattan, a happy queer princeling laden with new suedes and

silks and seersuckers and furs, ready to take up residence in a magical castle of my very own to rule over a glittering gay kingdom. I had a quiver full of glamorous, interesting friends, rising stars of the queer world whom I could now invite to the Greenwich Village townhouse Gramma had rented me for endless bohemian *salons* and Gatsby-esque galas. Omar had returned to my life during the previous year, no longer my lover but once again my best friend. I had a smart, sexy, and politically ambitious boyfriend who loved me, and a fall course load at NYU full of queer studies, history, poetry, and even *Introduction to Astronomy* for good measure. I had never felt so powerful, so invincible.

I'd put my time in being "good." Seventeen lonely years of it. Anyone who told me I was going too hard, too far, too fast could go to hell.

I was going to end up there eventually anyway, right?

BRAD

In New York, you found a new world of acceptance, freedom, and self-expression. It exacerbated the indignation you already carried toward Mom and me about what you saw as our repression of your sex life.

I was a professional representative of the Church, a theology teacher, and a former pastor. To you, I embodied a community where you were never able to be honest about yourself. Our conversations became more and more hostile.

During your first couple years in New York, you kept in touch regularly, calling me two or three times a week. Most of our phone calls were civil, sometimes even really enjoyable. Some were not. The most difficult phone calls became more frequent once you quit the musical theater program at NYU and began simply taking random classes that interested you. I remember a couple calls in particular that were intense. It felt like lasers of your anger sliced through my cell phone, losing not one degree of their searing heat over the 3,000 miles that separated us, as you responded to my "Hi, Drew" with tirades so loud that once I had to get up and leave the room, sure that my colleagues could hear you.

Can't I just "love the sinner but hate the sin?"

This is a common mantra that evangelicals use, perhaps because we believe it to be biblical, or perhaps because we feel like it makes us less judgmental. But it does not come across that way to most gay people, no matter how hard we explain it. To say we love them as a person while despising their behavior simply comes across as self-righteous rejection and condemnation. To understand why, we need to understand Stonewall.

Being openly gay in America has always been a risky thing, and in many ways it still is. But fifty years ago it was far more dangerous. In June of 1969, riots broke out in New York City when the LGBTQ community banded together to resist shakedowns and extortion after a police raid at the Stonewall Inn. Gay Pride parades were born to commemorate this event.

At Stonewall, LGBTQ people did not protest for the right to their sexual orientation. They protested for the right to be *open about it as public citizens. Thus for many gay people, to condemn their behavior simply communicates condemnation of them. Christians can argue all day long that that is not what we are doing, but it will still feel that way to gay folks. So if we want conversations to be productive, we should stay away from this line of reasoning.* —Brad

On the surface, I was the target of your anger. But below the surface, your fury was wider and deeper, roiling at the entirety of the evangelical culture I necessarily symbolized. I understood your anger, and shared some significant parts of it, regarding the unloving actions of those who proclaimed themselves representatives of evangelical America. But I also began to feel that the religious community you were describing was not the one I was part of. Instead, it was one identified only by its most radical and hateful factions. It was a caricature.

Foolishly, I attempted to argue with you about that. I tried to convince you that you were being unfair, that you were cherry-picking the worst of my world in order to condemn its entire population and purpose. That only made you more furious. Finally, I realized there were things going on that I couldn't understand, fanning your anger. I decided to back off until you could work through it.

DREW

While you were on the receiving end of those many angry phone calls, what you didn't see was the tenacity with which I was, at the same time, *defending* evangelicals against the onslaught of hate and defamation they received daily in my Queer Studies class.

"Intersections of Race, Gender, and Sexuality in US History," or just "Intersections" for short, was *that class* in my college career. The kind of esoteric but earth-shattering course you hear older people talk about decades later with reverent nostalgia because it changed their life.

Taught by Lisa Duggan, a brilliant, warm-yet-snarky cultural and political theorist who is a rock star of gay studies (with the leather miniskirts to match), "Intersections" was my game changer. Through the class, I began to accept myself and my sexuality in a whole new way—it was so wonderful. I felt that I'd been given permission to love myself exactly as I was, the privilege of dignity unsullied by the ever-present label of "brokenness." I felt like I was breathing clean air or drinking clean water for the first time. It's the kind of humanizing experience I wish upon every queer kid who grew up learning how to hate themselves for what they feel. I think it's what grace feels like.

Growing up, I had always been able to share my new feelings or discoveries with you and Mom. Now, however, you could not (or simply *would* not, as I felt about it at the time) rejoice with me in what I was learning. My emergent sense of dignity was not something I felt I could call and gush about. This caused me great sadness, which quickly morphed into resentment and contempt.

Looking back now, in spite of the new things I was learning, I think that deep down I still felt I needed to be punished and condemned for my homosexuality. That habit dies hard. If my own conscious brain couldn't do it, I would make my family—you and Mom and Breegan and Corey—do the flogging for me. My internalized feelings of disgust, revulsion, and rejection were transferred onto the four of you. I began to make you into the evil adversaries I needed you to be, often at the precise moments when you were just trying to love, support, and understand me to the best of your ability and without judgment.

With this newfound ability to turn more powerful and sophisticated lenses on my life experiences, I felt able to give names to feelings and ideas that had up until then been inexpressible. I now had a whole new language for telling you exactly why evangelical Christians were the worst thing to happen to humanity since The Black Death, hemorrhoids, or reduced-fat milk.

I remember how excited I was when the first book Professor Duggan assigned us was *The Family*, Jeff Sharlet's exposé (the size of *Moby-Dick*) on "The Secret Fundamentalism at the Heart of American Power." All throughout Sharlet's muckraking tome, I came across people from whom I was separated by only one or two degrees, and organizations I had known and interacted with all my life. I got a huge rush when I could raise my hand (from my seat in the back of the lecture hall, draped in a floor-length arctic fox fur coat and shielded behind my "ironically" cheap plastic sunglasses) to talk about my first-hand experience with the very people we were studying. Yes, indeed, I had lived among the chimpanzees and known their subtle ways, somehow making it out the other end to arrive here, in the land of humankind.

"Should I change how I act around my LGBTQ kid?"

Evangelical Christians want our faith not to be just a "Sunday thing," but something that guides us in every area of life. Putting faith on the back burner is not an option. To do so would mean being untrue to who we are.

In our family, this meant we were regularly involved in and talking about Christian aspects of our lives. Once Drew left the church and became openly gay, I became acutely aware that the habits of our Christian life were probably irritating to him. I wondered if they would cause him to want to spend less time with us. But at the end of the day, Robin and I decided that just as Drew wants us to accept him for who he is, we need to be accepted on the same terms.

So whatever your life of faith looks like, my advice is to stay true to that. Don't stop talking about God, community, and the other things connected to your faith. Don't stop praying at the table when your gay adult child is there. If it is Christmastime and your gay adult child no longer goes to church, tell him the family is going to Christmas service and ask if he would like to come—no pressure. Then it's their decision. Let them make it, and don't worry about it one way or the other. In short, live out your faith when your adult gay child is with you in basically the same way you do when they are not. —**Brad**

This was fun for a while. But then something deep inside my gut began to churn—and not just because I'd killed ten cigarettes and three espressos before seminar. As I listened to my classmates— many of whom were brilliant and highly informed on the evangelical Christian Right and its influence on the nation—talk disparagingly about the people I had grown up with, the village that had raised me, the big-hearted women who served in our church's low-cost clinic and sent me birthday cards every February, I began to feel . . . what, *defensive? Protective? Indignant* even? Surely not.

But the feelings grew.

In class, I began to take the part of the evangelical Christians who until then I had delighted in exposing, ridiculing, lamenting. I found myself fighting the monolithic, one-dimensional way in which all evangelical Christians were portrayed as wicked. Perhaps what began to get me the most upset was the continuing portrayal of all American evangelicals as cretins who had no knowledge of culture, no appreciation of art, and no ability to nuance their understanding of reality with anything beyond a black-and-white vision of the world. This picture was not consistent with our family, or any of the families we were close to growing up, all of whom were intellectuals who could discuss the great literature and ideas of the world over dinners that didn't include a *single* casserole.

I started to speak up.

Naturally, I was not about to let *you* know this shift was happening. In fact, it was necessary for me to step up the intensity of my weekly phone beatings, my condemnation now swollen with the lexicon of critical queer theory and a laundry list of examples of how evangelicals have massively screwed up. Plenty of these grievances I threw at your doorstep were legitimate, such as 2014's so-called "Kill the Gays" bill in Uganda (drafted by rogue members of Exodus International and financially supported by American evangelicals). But I was never interested in giving you space to respond to these systemic problems. Rather, they took the form of vicious diatribes against you personally.

I became consumed by defensiveness, primed to explode anytime I was around our family. I flew into a rage at any comment from Breegan that I perceived to have the *slightest* sense of disapproval of gay life. I made sweeping, inaccurate declarations about how she found all homosexuals "disgusting," how she believed we could not be moral people, how she secretly, deep-down, thought that I and those like me were destined for *hell*. I made patronizing references to her faith or her Christian friends, assassinating their characters and telling her what I knew they "really" thought of me.

Breegan's effort to understand my life and ask questions was often met with vicious accusations and barbs.

Once I said to Mom, my voice full of indignant heartbreak, "Do you know what it feels like for me to be unable to tell you that I've met someone who I care about and who cares about me? That part of my life I cannot include you in at all, unlike your normal, righteous, *unbroken* children! Do you understand what that feels like?"

Love, acceptance, and participation in life does not mean "agreement." If you have had clear thoughtful conversations about your religious convictions, acceptance of your child's partners and participation in their life will not make them assume you have changed your views.

Again and again, Robin and I have found that our decision to embrace Drew's gay friends and partners has never, and I really mean never, led Drew nor his friends to come to the conclusion that we agree with the way they live out their lives sexually. Drew is always very clear with his friends about who we are and what we believe before he introduces them to us, which understandably produces significant fear and suspicion in them.

But embracing them has created bridges for relationship that have allowed some of his friends and partners to believe that a person can have conservative Christian beliefs about homosexuality and still love and embrace them exactly as they are, which, I believe, is how God engages all of us, the whole world, in Christ. Embracing Drew's partners has not compromised our Christianity, but it has allowed Robin and me to welcome into our lives some delightful, intelligent, and engaging persons who have made our lives richer. —Brad

Mom had never *once* told me I couldn't share these things with her. In fact, her response to me at the time was to say, albeit still with some trepidation, that actually she would *like* me to tell her these things. My own self-hatred, however—my deep fear of having disappointed you through my failure to make a successful "conversion" in ex-gay therapy—would not allow me to believe her. In my own mind, I could not share the authentic joys of my committed relationship to my boyfriend because they were dirty, unclean, and unfit for my perfect mother; so my resentment turned on her and I attacked her for things she had never felt nor said.

This was how I kept my sanity. I felt it necessary to harden my approach toward you all in order to allow myself the space to defend you in my classroom.

It was a strange duality, this double role of "Defender of the Faith" to my school friends and "Queer Crusader" to my family. It left me lonely, furious, uncomprehending, and sad. Surrounded by book after new exciting book, ensconced in the joyous haze of booze and marijuana smoke and conversation that permeated the four rambling floors of my Bleecker Street townhouse, it seemed like the more I came to understand for certain, the less I seemed to know for sure.

BRAD

The biting, hostile calls were always balanced by those where you pleaded with me to find a way to be part of your world, the place where you finally felt welcomed for who you were. If you could still be a "Defender of the Faith" in a Queer culture so hostile to my Christianity, a stance for which you clearly paid a price with your peers, couldn't I surrender a *small* doctrine of my faith that kept me from fully approving of your life?

Wasn't our relationship worth some pushback from my evangelical peers?

Of course, from where I stood, it wasn't my peers that concerned me; it was my God.

Where the argument always hit a snag was when I would tell you that I loved you unconditionally and accepted you as my gay son. For you, unless I could tell you that I was totally *fine* with gay sex, you could never really believe that I accepted you for who you were. I remember telling you that my love would compel me to go as far toward you as I could, but that it was not right for you to ask me to violate my conscience, a conscience shaped by a morality that was above me.

So many times during those conversations, I thought of Chaim Potok's *The Chosen* and the relationship between Rabbi Saunders and his brilliant son, Danny, who did not want to follow in the religious ways of his ultra-Orthodox Jewish father. The narrator told a story from the Mishna about a father and a son who were hopelessly separated over some kind of life issue. Finally, the father said to the son, "You come toward me as far as you can go, and I will come the rest of the way." The problem was that *I* was the one who felt I could only go so far. How I *wished* I could go all the way to where you were! But I could not. In the long run, it really ended up being you coming to *me*, after I had come as far as I could.

Kids, you need to come to grips with the fact that your parents may never fully embrace who you are in a way that is satisfying or that makes you feel truly accepted, despite what might be their most sincere efforts. This was something that took me years to admit, and is still something I struggle with every day. The struggle, for me, can be so enraging and so painful, that some days it makes me feel like I can hardly face my life at all. The reason, of course, is the depth of my affection for my parents—not only as the humans to whom I owe my existence, but because I enjoy them as individuals. I love them so much.

We choose our deepest friendships. But we do not choose our families. Facing the fact that the way you experience love and romantic desire is designated by your family's system of beliefs to be tremendous, deadly sin . . . that realization can cause huge pain and profound anger.

Out in "the real world," we would not typically choose a friendship—a core level, sustaining, and abiding friendship—with someone whose belief system seems so hostile to our identity. It would be too hard. But I believe we have the opportunity to gain great value through maintaining our relationships with our parents and extended families in spite of their differing beliefs—value that can enrich our existence to a level often worth the price we pay for it. —**Drew**

This took about two years for us to work out. I remember one phone call that made me face the fact that I simply had to move toward you in a way that was uncomfortable for me if we were going to make any progress. It was a weekend, and I was sitting in my closet talking to you on the phone. We had been going back and forth about my moral scruples about gay sex when you asked me, "Look, Dad, would you rather have me in a long-term, monogamous relationship with a man who really *loves* me, or would you prefer I be having sex with a different guy every night who I don't even know?"

Some topics can't be addressed productively until some time has passed. For us, conversations about causes of Drew's sexuality, for example, did not work for several years. (Here's why: if you focus on cause, your child will perceive this as your attempt to "fix" them. Your child becomes a project, like repairing the dry rot in the deck so it can be safely enjoyed again by family and friends. Press this far enough and your kid will feel that the only way you will really love them is if they stop being gay.) We were eventually able to talk about his ideas around what causes different sexualities, but it was after several years and it was he who brought it up, not me.

I think it is really important to talk about the process you are going through personally with things like acceptance, fear, guilt, moving toward each other, etc. For most evangelical parents, the journey of embracing your gay child is one filled with lots of barriers. The point is not to pretend those barriers don't exist, but to figure out how to keep them from obstructing a loving relationship. —**Brad**

Neither of those options were on my top ten list. But I realized that I was not the one coming up with the options. You were.

"That's a no brainer, Drew," I answered. "Of course I would rather have you in a faithful relationship with someone who really loves you. You deserve to be loved, and at the end of the day, loving relationships are the only things that matter."

That was the moment we finally began to move back toward each other.

I was simply going to have to allow my expectations to be reshaped if we were going to preserve our relationship.

For some gay adult kids, keeping their everyday gay relationships separate from the world of their conservative families feels like the solution most conducive to peace. I would never judge that decision, but I think so much can often be gained when parents meet one of their gay child's significant others—or even significant friends—whom they find they can really get along with. It humanizes the whole conversation.
—Drew

Around the time of that phone call, you began a steady relationship with Austin, a bright, ambitious young man in New York. It was also at that time that you, Breegan, and Corey secretly planned to send your mom and me to New York City for our twenty-fifth anniversary. Since you all had very little in the way of financial resources for such an endeavor (Breegan and Corey were poor teenagers and Gramma Patti's financial help did not mean you were always flush with cash—not with your spending habits!), you secretly emailed dozens of our friends and family, shamelessly asking them to contribute to a fund for our flight and for spending money and tickets to Broadway shows. Accommodations would be free at your house in the Village, of course. But those accommodations meant that we were not just going to be staying with you, but with you and Austin.

You were a couple.

Your turf.

Your life.

Your rules.

Visiting your child and their partner is one of those moments when evangelical parents of gay kids often really struggle. Perhaps the thought process goes something like, "For goodness sake, isn't it enough that in order to stay in relationship with my son I have been willing to live with the fact that he is gay? And when it comes to sleeping arrangements, at least I have some control over my own world and my own home. But if I go into his world, am I really going to have to endure staying in the same house with him and his partner too? What if they HAVE SEX while we're there?"

Well, for many evangelical parents, that is exactly what staying connected to your gay son or daughter will mean. It was that phone call and your gritty, pointed question that made it possible for your mom and me to decide that is what it would mean for us. Given only two options, we would much rather you share your life and your intimacy with someone who was in your life every day and really cared about you than to share it with men who might not even have the time to learn your name. —Brad

But entering into your life, truly being part of your world, meant more than just staying in your house with you and your partner. When you were growing up, one of the ever-present qualities of our home life was laughter. At least half of the tears we shed around the dinner table were because of a joke you told, a hilarious story Breegan relayed in her prim deadpan, or one of those quirky uses of grammar or vocabulary that could only come from Corey. But after you went to New York, Mom and I did not laugh as much when we were in your world. Humor was as much a part of your life as an adult gay man as it had been as a kid in our home—and your friends were funny as well! But sometimes the humor was "gay humor." Mom and I didn't laugh at that. It's not that it wasn't *funny*, but it was "gay funny." Laughing was difficult for us because it was humor that came from a world that challenged our moral convictions and, maybe even more important, for us it was humor that always came with pain.

Parents, if you are going to stay connected to your LGBTQ kid, you need to look for the reflections of God's love in their life, even in places that might be difficult or uncomfortable—relationships with significant others or even the queer community at large. In spite of disagreement, can you celebrate things you see as beautiful in these relationships? There can be kindness, humor, care, commitment, and sacrifice even in the places none of us expect. To use some beautiful language from Christianity, "the image of God" can consistently be found in places we don't expect to find it. Worth and love can be seen even in the actions of those with whom we disagree. —Drew

We talked on the phone about it. I don't know how we got onto the topic, but you said, "Dad, I really need to ask you to lighten up when you are with me and my friends. You never laugh at our jokes and stories when they are about being gay. I know that it's uncomfortable, even painful for you. But most of the richest humor in the world comes out of pain, Dad. It's painful to be gay in this world—especially in the Christian world, which will always be part of my heritage. Sometimes we need to laugh just to deal with the pain. *Laugh* with us, Dad. It doesn't matter if you agree with homosexuality. Just *laugh*."

I saw the truth in what you were saying. Those phone calls freed me to love you better, to embrace Austin, and to *laugh*.

Chapter Eight

THE LAST
FIVE YEARS

BRAD

The last stage of your life in New York was difficult for two
reasons—the fear of HIV and the reality of drugs. The young
gay male community in New York has many, many sides. To be
fair, it's important to say there is no single "gay community,"
or "gay lifestyle," and the common depiction of gay people—
especially gay men—as morally bankrupt, sexually promiscuous
gadabouts is the kind of defamation often engaged in by those
who don't actually have relationships with any flesh-and-blood
gay people. That being said, there is a very real side of New
York's gay male world where anonymous hookups involving
dangerous quantities of alcohol and drugs are common.

You were never one to just put your toes in the water of life's
experiences, so you were *all* in, fully in a life that Mom and I
knew wasn't just against our morals, but objectively dangerous
for your health. We worried about you.

Your kid's health should not be ignored. If they are old enough to be sexually active, part of parental love is having difficult conversations focused on their well-being. HIV is not the death sentence it used to be, thank God. But it is still a very serious health threat that changes a person's life forever. Honesty is needed. A recognition of each other's fears. No condemnation or lectures.

Also important is that you ask your gay kid about their health in ways that are not always about HIV. Talk to them about their health in the same way you talk to your other kids; recognize the hurt caused over past decades by the insensitive and politicized ways that evangelicals in particular have treated the disease. —Brad

Misconceptions about HIV have been extremely damaging in my own life. These often become internalized by many who, like me, come from religious backgrounds. One of the effects of this can be a certain fatalism that HIV/AIDS is inevitable, often manifesting in high risk or self-destructive sexual behavior. Today there are more ways than ever before to protect against HIV infection, including medication that nearly prevents the possibility of HIV transmission. Because gay men are in a higher risk group for transmission than the general population—as are hemophiliacs, health care workers, and anyone who lives in Africa—they need to take precautions. Talking intelligently and lovingly with your kids about HIV risk and self-care is a sure way to make them feel valued. Kids, gay or straight, should be as informed as possible about their sexual health and risk, and should talk with their parents about it. Get checked regularly, and explain to your parents the relationship you have to your sexual health, including if contracting HIV becomes a part of your life. This world is full of danger and uncertainty. No one can be sure of what will happen to them tomorrow; even the Bible tells us that. What we can be sure of, however, is the love and support of those in our families who we trust. Tell your parents that this love and support, more than anything, is the most important thing they can offer you. —**Drew**

Those phone calls we had with you after you had just been to a free clinic to get checked out after exposure to HIV were no fun. You were worried. We were afraid for you.

During those years, I came to hate the sound of the phone ringing. It's not that I didn't want to talk to you. I did. But I was scared that I'd pick up the phone one day and hear you tell me, "Dad, I'm HIV positive." Sometimes I just sat at my desk at work and wondered, *What would I say to him? His life will be changed forever and there will be nothing I can do to help him.*

I thought about the loneliness you endured as a child, and found myself longing for those days rather than living with the specter of HIV/AIDS anywhere near my boy. But I knew that the pain of your childhood was in some ways at the heart of why you were living a life that now even you would call reckless and dangerous. I would have done anything in those days to change the way you were living, to protect you, to make you safe. But the only thing I could do was keep loving you. And pray.

DREW

I hear your love, Dad, but the fear of HIV/AIDS that you express as a parent now would piss off a lot of my gay friends over forty. Here's the feeling:

"First of all, *Reverend,* you know nothing about 'living with the specter of HIV/AIDS.' While my friends were dying gruesome deaths all around me as I watched in despair, terrified to even *kiss* anyone, you were still voting for Ronald Reagan, sheltered from the horror that was our daily lives, participating in the political machine that ignored us, condemned us, and withheld funding for scientific research and basic care from us. The fact that your son slept with half of New York twenty-five years later in an age when HIV in America for the medically insured isn't so much different than living with diabetes *gives you no insight whatsoever* into what it's like to 'live with the specter of HIV/AIDS.' I lived with that specter for a decade and by the grace of God survived it, all while you and your community were happy to let us die because we 'deserved' what your hateful God had 'sent' us."

Christians sometimes cringe at bitterness from "angry homosexuals," but if they don't care to look at the historical realities behind that anger and hurt, they're not impressive to me as Jesus-followers. I thought about this constantly during my later years in New York, as I studied the history of HIV/AIDS in America. The sadness and anger that grew in my soul found expression in more and more reckless patterns of behavior.

BRAD

It's important for me to hear those feelings, Drew. You are right; I was ignorant of much of the horror the gay community endured during those years. Honestly, much of the evangelical community then had the attitude that HIV/AIDS was a "gay disease," the consequence for irresponsible sexual behavior.

It wasn't our issue. Or so we told ourselves.

There is a tremendous stigma associated with HIV-positive people, one that is ugly and socially destructive. This stigma can be as present within the gay male community as it is without. But something that conservative Christians need to reckon with is an awful history of their community calling HIV things like "God's plague on wicked sodomites." This characterization from Christians bears real political responsibility for the lack of funding and research for AIDS during the decade in which it emerged, the years of the Reagan administration and the Moral Majority. The Reagan administration's disgust for gay people fueled their aggressive blocking of the gay community's pleas, as well as the outcries of scientists—many of whom were Christians themselves—for attention and funding to fight the disease during the years when AIDS could have been brought under control. The behind-the-scenes attitude of the Reagan administration, and the public attitude of the outspoken conservative Christian groups of the day, was to "let those faggots die."

Today, AIDS has a forty-million-body death toll, most of whom are not gay men, but mothers and children in Africa and the Global South. The gay men dying in the 80s didn't matter to the conservative Christians in power, so there was no money or political will to bring the disease under control. But now it's a raging global epidemic striking mostly at people whom evangelicals traditionally do care about, whose deaths do matter. The irony is sad, and infuriating for both gays and many Christians.

Parents should learn and consider this history. It's fine for them to be concerned about the higher level of HIV/AIDS risk which studies show that gay men face. But they need to know the context. —Drew

Toward the end of your time in New York, I began to understand your life was in trouble. It was a May phone call that convinced me I needed to get on a plane the next day and go be with you. Thankfully, classes had just ended for the semester. I was in the middle of a week of grading papers, but I had the flexibility to leave work for a few days.

Since this book is about the homosexuality side of our journey, I will not spend much time talking about the drug side. But your life in New York included a connection to drugs, a connection that continues to haunt you.

It was during that visit with you that you explained to me that one component of that scene in New York City, as well as other major American cities, was crystal meth. To make a long story short, you were beginning to realize that this part of your life had become too much to handle, at least on your own in Manhattan.

DREW

Crystal and I, we go pretty far back.

When I was eighteen, within a month of arriving in New York, I was on another plane flying home to the land of my childhood to bury my cousin Marie in the soft Missouri dirt. She had died as the result of an accident in a house where her friends were cooking crystal meth, a drug she had known for years.

Your sister's daughter had been like an older sister to me, Breegan, and Corey. Marie was delicate and fierce, a stunning blonde wild card with a cynical sense of humor who treated all of us kids with deep tenderness. We had passed the summers and holidays of our childhoods with Marie and her big brother, the pack of us cousins roaming wide across your mom's bucolic Midwestern farm full of hay bales and tractor trailers.

I respected Marie. I knew about her struggles with addiction, but beyond that I was always grateful that she had been the only person in our family, besides you and Mom, to whom I had disclosed my sexuality in the years before I came out. It happened on an autumn night, sitting on the back balcony of her house in Missouri. There was no moon in the sky, and we could see our breath. Marie was smoking Parliament cigarettes, and, since I had attained the ripe old age of fourteen by then, she let me have one. I felt that I could be honest with her, and I told my big cousin Marie about my "SSA" predicament. I explained, using my best ex-gay logic, how the pain and rejection I had experienced as a boy had given rise to this "damaged and broken" sexuality. I was careful to make clear that I was taking all the necessary steps to "deal with it."

She listened without interruption, and was silent for a long time. Then she turned to me and told me that everyone, *everyone*, is sexually messed up. No one gets through life without pain—pain we do nothing to earn, pain that happens to us. *Snap*. Like that. People hurt you. She told me that if I wanted to "fix" myself like I said I was trying to do—okay. Go ahead. But she also said that I might be a lot better off just accepting myself. She knew plenty of gay guys who were good people in loving relationships, and even some who loved Jesus. I was perfect, she said, just as I was. God could love me if I was gay. And so could she. At the time, I couldn't conceive of anyone else in our family responding like that. I took Marie's words and hid them in my heart.

Years later, in the months after I came out, Marie and I talked often. Having her support was wonderful. We were both the "problem kids" of our families, which meant we could laugh in the same ways at the same things. She promised to visit me in New York once I'd gotten settled. But less than a month after I arrived, she was gone.

The tragic way she died devastated us. It was a blow the three of us kids had never yet known in our lives. The depth of losing her made it feel impossible to *ever* divulge my own struggle with crystal meth once it had begun. That was a guilty secret I would never share with you and Mom. After what happened to Marie, no one could know.

The first two times I did crystal, I was tricked into it by guys who told me it was something else. I quickly realized I was a fan. The last two years of my five-year stay in Manhattan, I sought it often. For me the draw of crystal was always the sexual nature of how it's used within dark, warm corners of the gay world—taken to fuel marathons of sex with lots of partners in an environment of total abandon. Crystal is the one drug that can free me instantly, *deliciously*, from the sexual awkwardness and self-loathing I'm rarely without. When I'm high on crystal I feel nothing besides blissful, humming blankness and a total embrace of my physical being. I let loose. Crystal alleviates the shame of trauma, at least for the moment, and that's what's awesome about it.

What's less awesome about crystal is that with the tremendous rush, inhibitions vanish, which often means high-risk sex, often with significantly higher incidences of HIV and STD infection. Now, HIV today is not the kind of death sentence it was when you were my age in the 80s. But contracting it is still a serious life issue, and I know that it caused you and Mom many sleepless nights during my latter New York years. You may not have known about the drugs, but you knew about the times I went into the clinic for tests, scared because my odds of having contracted HIV were a lot higher than I wanted them to be.

I have to say, though, that there has always been a somber secret at the core of my risk-taking with meth and sex: a part of me *wanted* to contract HIV.

Within this "unthinkable" desire was a death wish: the Christian moralist inside me knew I needed to be "punished." Add to this the consideration—no small one, given how overwhelming HIV/AIDS has been for thirty years in the American Gay psyche—that seroconversion (becoming HIV positive) has the effect of instantly releasing a person from the fear of contracting it. Many gay men fear HIV contraction so mortally, that a part of you just wants the agony of seroconversion-phobia to be over with already.

> *Parents, ask questions about your son or daughter's relationships, both friendships and romantic connections. I remember a telephone conversation with Drew where he said to me, "Dad, when I am in a relationship with someone, you never ask me about it. If Breegan or Corey are in a dating relationship, you ask how things are going because you care about them. Can you see how that might make me feel? Dad, if our relationship is going to move forward, you need to ask me about the men I am dating."*
>
> *For many evangelical parents, the response might be, "So am I supposed to want my child to prosper and be happy in a relationship that I believe is wrong?" I guess the answer to this question depends on your perspective about whether or not you believe that staying in positive, loving relationship is the best way to the best outcomes for your child. If you believe that suffering is the best way to move your child in that direction, then you will not want them to find anything truly*

redemptive and good in their gay relationships, which will definitely lead to increased suffering for them. But given the enormous rate of depression and suicide among young gay people today, I suggest that increasing their suffering for their homosexuality is a dangerous approach. —Brad

One could label this "fatalism," I guess, but it's a fatalism that comes from the environment we grew up in: Gay Sex = Death. This was true in a religious sense before AIDS entered the picture ("He who lies with a man as with a woman shall be put to death"), but the morbid equation became viciously real after 1982, as conservative Christian America gleefully pointed the finger at "God's Curse" on homosexuals while their own gay sons died in droves.

Finally, and perhaps most paradoxically, I wondered deep within me if contracting HIV wouldn't make me a better person. A braver person. A more morally engaged and less useless person. Having craved adventure from the time I was young, romanticizing the ideal of a self-sacrificing hero who disciplines his body and mind to fight on behalf of the oppressed and the just causes of the world, it made me sick and ashamed to see the self-indulgent man I had become, living the life of a spoiled New York princeling. Contracting HIV would be—oh God, mightn't it just be?—the kind of life-and-death-level change that could spur me into principled action. A ticking time bomb forcing me to make the best use of my energies and days on earth.

I still think about this.

Being a gay child in conservative evangelical America is its own kind of trauma, and being sexually "re-educated" from age twelve to seventeen is traumatic. In order to be a conscious, ethical human, you have to find a way to transcend personal trauma and transform it into a life well lived. But that road isn't simple. It's riddled with perils for mind, body, and soul.

BRAD

When we were on the home stretch of finishing this book, several of my colleagues asked me, "Was writing this book with Drew healing for you guys?"

"No," I've said. "Drew and I did most of our healing a few years ago. Writing this book has transported both of us back to relive some of the worst moments of our lives. Honestly, it has been emotionally brutal." Talking with my counselor recently about the depression I have been fighting as we come to the end of the project, I was able to put into words something that I'm sure other Christian parents of gay kids have felt.

I have to face the fact that *I* am one of the reasons you experienced trauma, Drew.

When I was a young man, I swore that my kids would never have to face the pain I felt from my alcoholic father, who I knew loved me, but was so wrapped up in his addiction and self-hatred that he simply could not be a significant part of my life or make me a part of his. So from the time you kids were little, I have done my best to be at every theater production, every soccer and volleyball game, and to make sure you knew that you were a huge part of what made my life beautiful. But in your case, when all was said and done, there was a part of you I could never fully accept. Caught between my religious convictions and my promise to my kids, I have ended up being a source of disconnection in our relationship after all.

DREW

By my third year in New York, my secret struggles with meth had begun to come to a head, though on the surface my life seemed idyllic. I worked for an independent filmmaker who was one of my greatest mentors, and my Bleecker street townhouse pulsed with the artists and writers, socialites, and rebellious runaways who formed a communal ecosystem around that magical palace. Gramma Patti dropped in every few months in a blaze of glory, partying with the young New Yorkers who found her so irresistible (and most of whom she could out-drink). By that point I had dropped out of NYU, I was working on a screenplay, and was surrounded by glittering entertainment professionals who stroked my ego. The life I led seemed the definition of fabulous.

But secretly, I was spiraling further into a perilous darkness, terrified that anyone might find out where I disappeared to every few months for days at a time.

Marie appeared to me in my dreams, as she has to all three of us kids over the years. She was often far away. Then something happened that brought her close to my waking world in a way I could never have foreseen.

"But secretly, I was spiraling further into a perilous darkness."

After breaking up with Austin, the only long-term boyfriend I had ever had, I dated a string of men, but nothing stuck. As my weekend binges became separated by fewer and fewer months, then weeks, I became increasingly sure there was no way I would ever have a meaningful relationship. *I'm garbage*, I felt inside, *but nobody knows.* Then I met Elliot.

It will be odd for you, at first, when your gay or lesbian child comes to you and says, "Dad, (significant other) and I are really struggling with resolving conflicts in our relationship right now. How have you and Mom dealt with that over the years? I need some advice." At this point, I suggest you swallow hard, remember that staying in relationship matters most in this journey, and help your child with his desire to be a better partner.

Of course this commitment to engage your child's friends and partners will result in challenging questions: Can they stay at your house? Will you go to their wedding? If so, will you participate? I cannot answer these questions for anyone but myself. So my advice is simply this: always opt for positive relational connection as long as it does not compromise anyone's understanding of your principles. —Brad

Elliot was beautiful, brilliant, and utterly bewitching. He's the kind of man who becomes the center of all stares the minute he enters a room. Because he'd grown up in Missouri, we had a shared sensibility that delighted both of us. We could talk for hours about trivial gossip, or Marxism and Malcolm X. After a few months I found that I had fallen for Elliot harder and faster than anyone before, ever. I was enraptured and infatuated with this young man and sure of my desire to be with him and *only* him.

One night the two of us were sitting on the roof at Bleecker Street, and I decided that if Elliot and I were to have a real relationship, the kind I felt unworthy of but so desperately wanted, it had to be with the knowledge of my deep, shameful secret. I told him, as vaguely but as sincerely as I could manage, that I had struggled "in the past" with using crystal meth. He listened, and was quiet for a long time.

Meeting my eyes steadily with his, Elliot told me that hearing this was extremely hard for him, because meth had marked his family in a terrible way. His adopted brother had gotten involved with it in the Missouri town where they lived. Then one night, a girl was in his house, and an accident happened. She died tragically shortly after, and Elliot's brother was now in jail for a sentence lasting decades, in part because of this girl's death.

I stared at him, and as I felt the universe closing in around me, I asked him if the girl who died was named Marie.

She was.

My precious cousin was gone, and Elliot's adopted brother was behind bars, and there the two of us sat on a Manhattan rooftop in the freezing dark, thousands of miles away from our families whose lives had been ripped apart by the tragedy we had no idea connected us.

Words become inadequate at the moments our lives pass through the veil separating the dead and the living. Reaching across from the other side was Marie. I felt her in that moment, and I felt God. I had no idea what they were saying to me, other than, *We're here with you. We see you. You are not alone.*

Elliot and I stopped dating shortly afterwards. My heart was broken, and the shame I felt for the inexplicable connection between us was like a secret cancer. That winter I moved through New York in a daze, haunted by what had happened and my inability to make sense of it. The work I'd been putting into my screenplay piddled off into nil. I continued to coast on the money flowing into my account from Gramma Patti each month without question or condition. I redecorated the townhouse, bought clothes, threw parties, moved through meaningless flings, and continued to go missing every few weeks for days at a time on benders whose true nature I frantically hid from my friends and family.

BRAD

I don't know if our loved ones can reach back to us after they die, or if they know what is going on in our lives here on earth. I do believe Marie is with Jesus and she is safe, fully aware of how much she is loved. I also believe the grave is no obstacle for Christ, and whether or not what you felt was the actual presence of Marie, or simply your memories of her, God was using your deep love for each other as a means of telling you exactly what you heard: you are not alone in the universe; relationships are the only things worth living for. And when God sees our lives full of wreckage, He has powerful ways of letting us know He is there, walking beside us in the dark, even though we cannot see Him.

DREW

In the spring, several of my more sensible friends said flatly, "Drew, you're a wreck. Go get a job." Thankfully, I listened. Among the various gigs I worked that summer was as an assistant to an Oscar-nominated documentarian. He was making a film about Egyptian heavy metal musicians who'd been swept up into the Arab Spring Revolution, and toward the end of the summer I bought a ticket to go with him to Cairo to shoot some more footage. But in the week before I was scheduled to leave, I screwed up a major job I was supposed to do for him—because I'd been high on a bender. He called me, screaming.

"You're a nice person," he bellowed, "but you've got a lot of f***ing problems, you're clearly a drug addict, and that woman in Portland who gives you all that money hasn't done you any f***ing favors! You're going to have to learn to grow up some day and live in the real world—but you're not going to do it on my time!"

He was right and I knew it. I set off for Egypt on my own, huffing and indignant. *This is even better*, I thought. *Now I can have an adventure without some jerk telling me what to do all day long.* A deeper part of me, the part that saw what my life had become and was frightened, knew that when I'd gone to Egypt as a young man I had found something there, something that had set me free and altered the direction of my life. I wondered if it was possible to find that again. Still reeling from the visitation I had felt from Marie months before, I was desperate for a chance to wrench myself free from New York.

My three-week vacation in Egypt turned into three months, and it wasn't so much a vacation as a beautiful and brutal reeducation. In September 2011, the Revolution had been raging since January. The months I spent immersed in that foment of sacrifice and upheaval for the ideal of freedom altered my heart. The young Egyptians I met, those who became and remain my closest friends, were the most inspiring and ethical people I've ever known. They were the kind of people I longed to be like—something for which I knew I had the capacity, buried somewhere under the glittering party monster I'd become.

During my time in Cairo, Gramma Patti came to visit. She charmed all of my Egyptian friends—"Drew's Gramma" is still legendary there. Many stories are told about the night this seventy-nine-year-old woman spent dancing with all the boys on a Nile yacht cruise in her glittering rhinestone abaya, or went trotting out to the pyramids on a camel in her striped silk hankie and Fendi shades—but it was the night of her arrival that I remember most.

I had spent the day preparing her suite at the Sofitel tower, placing flowers and pictures around to make it feel homey. Gramma's flight arrived at midnight from Amsterdam (where she'd been taking a merry tour of the city's canals, gardens, and Red Light District during her long layover), and I headed for the airport in one of the hotel's chartered cars. I had set up a little cocktail station in the back seat, complete with glasses, tonic, ice, expertly twisted lemon rinds, and a bottle of Grey Goose. As I was leaving the hotel, I began to see a flurry of activity on social media. Everyone in Egypt was talking about someone called "Maspero." Then it was talk of body counts, the military, and tanks flattening protesters under tread.

I soon realized that Maspero was not a person; it was a place downtown. Thousands of Egyptian Christians had marched there that evening, demanding a government response to the anti-Christian violence and burning of their churches sweeping through the south. The military had rolled in tanks and fired on the protesters. Twenty-eight people had been shot or flattened into human mush by tanks as they rolled over adults and children, and over two hundred were injured. It was the first anti-protester military violence in what had been

Drew and Gramma Patti at the Cairo Four Seasons, 2011.

177

until then a peaceful revolution, and as the massacre unfolded, Cairo descended into chaos.

On the ride to the airport, I frantically checked my Facebook and texted with my friends. I put on a welcoming smile as Gramma trotted out the causeway to my open hug, but inside I was sick to my stomach. As we tore through the emptied highways back to the hotel, we were stopped every few minutes at military check-points. I did my best to downplay the situation and keep Gramma entertained, but she wondered aloud why no one was on the road. I felt outside my body, watching from above as Gramma Patti and I laughed and cavorted in the back of the Mercedes, chilled imported vodka in hand, while the city literally burned.

This is my life, I thought. *The world is on fire with turmoil and issues of real importance, while I'm swilling overpriced booze in the back of a limousine.*

By the end of my time in Cairo, I knew that my days in New York would have to come to an end if I ever wanted to be a self-respecting human being again.

I wrote to our beloved landlord that week, telling him we would not be renewing our lease on the townhouse, and I applied to reenter school at Evergreen College back home in Washington. For my entire life, it felt, I had let others tell me who I was and what I could or couldn't do—either by following their words or by rebelling so hard against them that it was still their orders that ran my life, only in reverse. Now it was time to find out who I was on my own, a noble aspiration that came to a screeching, smoking halt in rehab two months later.

After crashing my college classmate's car while on a drunken bender to go find some crystal, I woke up in a hospital bed sur-rounded by you, Mom, and Breegan. During my high I'd called Corey while teetering on the edge of a bridge over Lake Union, ready to jump. My little brother's screaming sobs had begged me to climb down, but it was the cops who showed up to cart me to the hospital that got me off the edge. Corey didn't get over this for a long time. While you, Mom, Gramma Patti, and Breegan all came to visit me in rehab over the following month, Corey didn't. It was months before he spoke more than a few words to me, his eventual admission of terror and anger and love and sorrow flowing out in a long text message from a little brother to his big brother, whom he both idolized and resented for the way I'd endangered my life. Corey always keeps things so close, and when they eventually do come out it's in a rush of poetry that makes him the profound artist and brilliant songwriter he is. His popstar friends and industry colleagues all recognize this amazing quality as part of the reason Corey's so special, and I'll never forget that message he sent me.

Ultimately, it was about forgiveness.

BRAD

I was glad when I knew you were coming back home. I had missed you so much, and longed to live near you again.

When you arrived in the mid-summer of that year, you were not in good shape, physically or emotionally. The next six months were without question the rockiest we've ever had in our life with you. Most of the work was yours, of course, and you went through deep waters. Once you realized you were in over your head and had reached out for help, some great people came into your life to help you find a much better path.

After you emerged from rehab, we entered some of the best years we'd had for what felt like ages. 2013 and 2014 in Portland became years of watching you grow personally and in your professional craft. I'm so thankful that, even if it was just to get Mom to stop *bugging* you, you decided to audition for theater again. You took a leap of faith in returning to the thing that had given you so much pleasure as a young person, and the gates of opportunity were thrown wide.

DREW

Rehab was the first time since I was seventeen that I'd been sober for thirty days.

In my journey back to stability, I was carried by my family and by all those "church people" who had never condemned me or deserted me over the years. For the first time in many years, I slowly began to pray, though not *quite* to the God of my childhood. I watched the people in my 12-step programs, how they made the choice to come to God with the cares and joys of their daily lives, like I had been taught to do, but without making any claim to understand God any better than anyone else. I began to do the same. Often, when I prayed, I would talk to Marie, too.

I'm here, I'd tell her. *I know that I am not alone. I know that God can meet me where I am, as I am. Please help me see those things I ought not to miss. Let me see what I'm supposed to do.*

Usually, the answer I get, wherever it may be coming from, is *More Love, Less Fear.*

> *My kids would tell you that as they were growing up, the one thing I said to them more than anything else is that life is about relationships. If that is true, then it applies even to families torn apart by battles over sexuality. The only way to stay in relationship is to come to the table, again and again.* —Brad

When I came out of rehab, I had a long talk with Gramma Patti.

"Darling Fairy Godmother," I said, "you will always be my Gramma, but the sun has, I'm afraid, set on the days of patronage. It's time for Peter Pan to grow up and stop being such a Lost Boy." We cut up my credit cards together, and I moved into your and Mom's garage until I could afford a place of my own in Portland with money I earned myself, bussing tables. After achieving six months sober and financial self-sufficiency, I went on a theater audition, my first in five years, mainly to get Mom off my back.

"You were born for the stage, Drew!" she told me over and over again. "Just get out there!"

My first audition got me cast in *Threesome,* a brilliant, devastating new play by an Egyptian playwright being workshopped at Portland's big regional theater. It would eventually make its way to Seattle and a New York off-Broadway run. I couldn't have imagined a more perfect entree into the world of professional theater. It amused me wickedly that I spent the first half of the show buck naked; there I was, standing on a stage in front of six hundred people—including you and Mom and various members of your Bible study group—fully vulnerable and exposed in the service of a piece of ethically important art that I deeply believed in. As the audience, including my family, roared their applause at the final curtain, I felt I was finally standing on two feet as my own man in the world, unbowed (certainly "uncovered").

> *Kids: the same grace and broadness that my dad suggests to parents in seeing you as so much more than your sexual identity, I charge you to show to your parents. They are full and complex human beings beyond the limits of their conservative beliefs. One of the most beautiful experiences of my life has*

been watching my parents grow and change over the course of the years. I attribute a large part of that to my willingness to recognize their whole personhood, and my decision, over and over again, to represent them to my friends and the larger gay/secular world as more than "just" evangelical Christians.

I have chosen to introduce my parents to my friends—gay and straight alike—as the people to whom I owe so many of my best attributes. This has helped them show me the same grace, and see in me a reflection of the good God they believe in. —Drew

After *Threesome* came an eighteen-month run of theater work—including *Fiddler on the Roof*, a beloved classic from my childhood; our hauntingly beautiful and unconventional vision of *A Christmas Carol* with me as Ebenezer Scrooge, the man given a second chance at life; *The Last Five Years*, a cautionary parable about a twenty-something writer's meteoric rise to fortune in New York and the cost of placing selfishness over relationship; and finally *Tick, Tick, Boom!*, a rock musical from the creator of *Rent* about a young man struggling to grow up and become an artist in the shadow of his own failures and HIV/AIDS. Each of these shows seemed like a divine gift—a part of my story.

BRAD

When I think about what has happened in our relationship since you came back from New York, what comes to mind is not new challenges or discoveries concerning how I need to relate to my gay son. We've had to work through some difficulties, but they have not had much to do with you being gay and me being an evangelical. Honestly, my concerns for you now go back to something much more basic, something in the heart of all Christian parents.

> Parents, my message is simple: don't ever give up. There will be times when you might want to. Don't. Your child may never agree with you. But they will never stop needing your love.
> —Drew

More than *anything*, I want you to know in your heart the love God has for you—to know you are of immeasurable value because He has created you to be in relationship with Him. But that is not something I can control. We have been through all the intellectual discussions about the existence of God and the credibility of the biblical story, and we simply disagree. Further reasoning will not change that for either of us. Your relationship with God is between you and Him.

I'm glad when the beauty of worship still draws you to church with us on occasion. Those mornings you come, I have no expectations. I'm just happy. I love it when you stand next to me, singing harmony to songs you still know as well as your name. I love how so many people who have known you since you were a boy hurry from across the room after the service so they can find out what you are up to. Sometimes it takes an extra hour to get to the car because so many people want to embrace you.

Perhaps what the last couple of years has taught me most is to accept you as an adult. You still felt like my child when you left for New York after high school. You are still my son, but you are not really my *child*. The more I conceive of you as an adult and the more I treat you like an adult, the stronger our relationship has become. I cannot control or change you. You are your own special creation.

I can't. And, actually, I don't want to.

It's way too much work at my age, when I find that so much of my energy is expended on getting a full night's sleep and trying to find the TV remote.

Parents, you need to come to grips with the fact that your child is gay, and the way they live their life may never change.

I was just talking with someone who told me that her lifelong best friend has a son who recently came out to them. They don't know what to do. She told me that they went to a presentation made by a Christian man and his gay son who told the story of the parents' prayer and the son's decision to live a celibate life because of his desire to follow Jesus. I know a number of stories like this one. Some of them are stories of gay Christians who decided either to live a celibate life or to enter a heterosexual marriage in order to enjoy the benefits of a traditional nuclear family. Some of them stayed true to their decisions for many years. And some of them are very happy. None of them, however, have "become straight." And as far as I am aware, they all still deal with attraction to persons of the same sex even after having been celibate or heterosexually married for years.

On the other hand, I also know many Christian families whose same-sex attracted kids have opted to live either multi-partnered or monogamous gay lives. Some of them, in the process, have left the church, and even their faith. Others have stayed

committed to the church and still identify as faithful follow-
ers of Jesus, believing that God is fine with them being gay
Christians.

Prepare yourself for a number of possible outcomes, espe-
cially as your child leaves the home to live an adult life. If
your adult gay child, out of a commitment to follow Christ,
decides to live a celibate or heterosexually married life, while
this decision may make you initially relieved, you had bet-
ter not think that things will now just "get back to normal."
A person who makes this choice is going to need enor-
mous support from family, church, spouse, and, later, even
kids. This person labors under a weight that few of us can
understand—a burden that often results in deep loneliness,
depression, and, for some, one or more forays into homo-
sexual encounters which then become the source of guilt,
broken relationships, and despair. So while this may be the
decision you want your son or daughter to make, and while
you will very likely believe it is the right decision and will
even be blessed by God, know that it usually comes with a
tremendous price. —**Brad**

We recently had a conversation about an issue in your life
of real concern to me. I wanted to tell you what I thought you
ought to do, but as the words neared my lips, I found myself
saying, "Drew, I'm not here to give you advice."

You responded, "Dad, it's okay. You're my father. I'm *asking*
you to give me advice."

Perhaps when we come to that place in our relationship,
we're in the best place we can be.

I hope we stay there.

DREW

I have always loved Robin Williams. From the time I was a kid watching him in movies like *Hook*, *Aladdin*, or our family favorite *Mrs. Doubtfire* (which my parents and siblings made me perform for them ad infinitum on road trips), I was drawn to his explosive, edge-of-your-seat energy that could conjure up an endless stream of what he called "people inside my head."

I met Robin once, if "met" is the right word. I was flying home from Maui, where I go every year with Gramma Patti. An accident of ticketing had me seated in the first row of business class instead of in coach. The plane was one of those giant airbuses with a business AND first class cabin, however—which meant that no matter how luxurious my flight was, I had a front row vision of how much *more* luxurious it might have been, if only I were just a little *more* important (this hanging carrot just out of reach is the "definitive characteristic of the bourgeois experience, the ferocious striving at the heart of capitalism"—at least that's what my journal notes from the flight say).

Robin Williams and his family took up the entire first class cabin. I watched him interact with his children and the airline staff as they returned from what seemed to have been a lovely family vacation. Everyone was happy and warm. I was in heaven.

We landed. Robin emerged from first class as I emerged from business, and we walked up the ramp side by side, my heart beating wildly. Suddenly an alarm went off in the airport, whining and screaming. He looked at me, and I rolled my eyes and said, "Oy vey."

He twisted his face up tight and in the voice of the Genie from *Aladdin* (when he takes the form of the Ace Pilot bumblebee) said, "Mayday, Mayday, MAYDAAAAYYYY!!!" and this was pretty much the climax of my life so far on earth. I treasured this tiny, insignificant interaction for months, giddily relating it to all my friends. I planned how I would tell him about this one day, when we were seated next to each other at the Academy Awards.

Six months later, Robin was gone.

I cried for days when I heard of his suicide. I've never had that kind of reaction to a celebrity's death. Mostly I was frightened. I heard that a bunch of my friends were watching marathons of his films to honor his work and life, but I couldn't even bring myself to watch the TV coverage that week. I have not wanted to watch a single Robin Williams movie since then, until recently. Dad was visiting me in New York, and in thinking about all the issues in this chapter, I decided we needed to watch *The Birdcage*.

In *The Birdcage*, Robin Williams and Nathan Lane play a middle-aged Jewish gay couple in Miami who own a drag nightclub. Their son comes home from college to tell them he's proposed to a beautiful girl. The girl's parents (Gene Hackman and Dianne Wiest) are on their way down to meet the family, which would be wonderful . . . if her father wasn't an arch conservative senator and cofounder of the "Society for Moral Order," dedicated to fighting the influence of liberalism, Jews, homosexuals, and everything else ruining America. At the son's insistence, his dad (Williams) removes anything "over-the-top" from their apartment (outrageous art, phallic sculptures, and pretty much all they own), to be replaced with the gothic minimalism of a monastery, right down to a giant crucifix hanging where the nude sculpture of Neptune used to stand. Williams changes out his flowered shirts and gold chains for a respectable suit, and locks Lane, the only "mother" his son has ever known, away for the evening.

The deception is awkward and unconvincing, and the senator

and his wife are suspicious of this young man with his nervous, laconic father, until suddenly "Mother" arrives in a blaze of glory—it's Nathan Lane, broken out of his imprisonment in flawless drag, right down to the honey blonde bouffant, pearls, and pink Chanel skirt suit. What follows is one of the best dinner parties in cinema. Hackman is charmed by Lane, seeing in 'her' the ideal "mother," committed to family values, prayer in schools, and good old-fashioned stand-by-your-man American womanhood; the two of them lead a rousing rendition of "I Could Have Danced All Night" while Williams and Weist play along on the piano. The common ground that Hackman and Lane's characters discover between them is real, the only difference being that Lane is not *technically* a woman, a minor detail that the senator and his wife fail to realize until the very end.

What stood out to Dad and to me as we watched this was how these two characters come together not *around* their worldviews, but *through* them—not *in spite* of them, but *by way* of them. This is ultimately how we hope gay children and Christian parents might interact.

Eventually, what happened for Drew, after years of wanting nothing to do with my Christian faith, was that he began to pray again with us—even asking if he could say the blessing at family meals. They were not the Christian prayers I had taught him as a boy. They did not end in the name of Jesus. Nevertheless, his heartfelt and tender thanksgiving to a nameless, faceless kind of electrical energy that somehow bonded us in mystical human union (like Chevy Chase and his golf balls in Caddy Shack), somehow still fills my heart with joy. —Brad

Neither party should stop being who they are to accommo-
date the other—doing so could squelch those opportunities to
find common ground between you in places you would have never
allowed yourself to look. While Williams and his son are doing their
best (and failing) to give the Senator and his wife what they're sure
they would want, Lane instead goes with what he does best—being
a genuinely caring and doting mother—and that *truth* is what the
senator resonates with.

I recently returned from a fourth trip to Cairo, where I wrote an
article for *GAYLETTER* (the queer magazine I work for in Manhattan) about sexuality in Egypt, and the perils of navigating that issue
in a place where things are—in certain ways—a lot dicier than here.

> *A viable, authentic adult relationship with your parents is
> worth the struggle. Because we never gave up on each other,
> and were willing to stay connected even when it was painful,
> we forged something amazing. The relationship I have with
> my parents now—a relationship between people with oppos-
> ing beliefs on a personal and important issue, who choose to
> affirm each other's humanity and dignity every day—is one of
> the most precious things I've experienced.* —**Drew**

During that trip, I thought often about how beautiful it is that
you and I can write this book, and how grateful I am to have gone
through this wild journey with *you*, and not someone else. When
Mom picked me up at the Portland airport, still covered in Cairo's
dust, and drove me to the Oregon coast to join you, my sister, my
brother, and our jolly little Gramma Patti, I couldn't wait to spend a
week with my evangelical Christian family.

How many gay kids, having been through what we've been through, could say that? Hopefully the work of this book is that a few more will know what that feels like. That they will come to know that disagreement doesn't have to mean disconnection.

We don't see the world the same way. But I can't imagine my world without you in it.

BRAD

Sometimes I think about the time you told Mom you did not like seeing Rembrandt's painting *The Return of the Prodigal Son* in our house. It made you feel guilty and uncomfortable, as if Mom and I saw you as our prodigal. So I moved the painting to my office at the university.

Honestly, I have never thought of you as a prodigal son. When I think about a prodigal, I think about a relationship that is totally, even if only temporarily, broken. Ours was never like that, thank God. But last summer you did something that let me know how much healing had taken place. After your performance in *The Last Five Years* closed, you stole one of the publicity posters hanging on the wall at Portland Center Stage. It was a life-size picture of you from the musical, standing on a table, belting out a high note. You handed it to me.

"Here, Dad," you said. "Hang this in your office next to the Rembrandt."

The irony was not lost on either of us!
It's still there.

EPILOGUE

BRAD

Twenty-six years ago, the doctor for Drew's surprise C-section lifted him up, bloody and beautiful. My life changed. Here was my son, my *boy*. I was taken, completely, in that cold delivery room. Words don't do the power of that moment justice.

Parents, you remember the first time you saw your son or daughter. You remember their smell, the sound of their cry, their need for you, so basic, so *different* than any relationship you had felt before.

You remember them growing up so fast, their milestones. Their words, their steps, their imaginary worlds. The books they asked you to read to them again, and again, and *again*. The first time something they said made you laugh. The first time something they said made you cry.

And if you're reading this book, you likely remember the moment you first suspected they were *different*.

That love we feel is founded on something strong enough to weather even our deepest disagreements. The bond between parent and child is special. It is, this theologian believes, something God made—something God knows and feels for every single person in the human family. It is holy, a love big enough for struggle, big enough for *different*. A love that can welcome another person in humility, a love so much deeper than bare "agreement" with a moral position or a lifestyle.

It's this love that the Apostle Paul writes about in the book of 1 Corinthians:

> *Love is patient, love is kind. It does not envy, it does not boast, it is not proud. It does not dishonor others, it is not self-seeking, it is not easily angered, it keeps no record of wrongs. Love does not delight in evil but rejoices with the truth. It always protects, always trusts, always hopes, always perseveres.*

This is the kind of love I, and all of us, need to receive. The kind we need to give in return.

I write these words as a man who loves Jesus and believes the Bible's teaching with my whole heart. But that same heart is full of seasoned, powerful love for my firstborn son. That love is like a seal upon my heart. Many waters cannot drown it.

It is my hope that reading our story has felt familiar to you. Every parent and child relationship is something unique and special. But there are also common things that we share, particularly when we struggle through an issue as deep and important as how a parent's belief and a child's sexuality intersect.

You have your own story, your own road forward with your child. Wherever that leads, it is my prayer to God for you that you find—and make—space for faith. Space for humility. Space for love. Space at your table.

I invite you to that love. It can deepen, perhaps even save, your relationship with your beloved child.

Space at the table has done that for Drew and me.

DREW

On a recent family trip to the beach, I sat overlooking the Oregon coast with my parents. As I watched the teal silver waves all trimmed in crisscrossing lace like some Edwardian gown, Neil Young's song "Helpless" started crowing out of the music player. For the first time in years, it struck me that the song's chorus, in its cadence and chords, sounds a lot like the worship songs I sang as a kid. Without a thought, I found myself harmonizing, like I would have on any Sunday morning. I resisted the urge to close my eyes and lift my hands.

The American evangelicalism I grew up in, like any all-encompassing religious tradition, is a language. You can stop speaking it, you can try your best to forget it, but you can't unlearn it. Thankfully, I long ago stopped trying.

All my friends in Cairo have printed on their state-issued ID card their name, date of birth, marital status, and religion—Muslim or Christian. Almost none of my Cairene friends have meaningful religious convictions either way, but that's beside the point; in Egyptian culture, your religion as a marker of identity goes beyond the piddling confines of individual credo. My Egyptian friends understand—in a way that my Manhattan friends raised in secular-humanist homes can't quite grasp—what I mean when I say, "Once an evangelical, always an evangelical."

About a year ago, I found myself in Egypt to stage a reading of Yussef El Guindi's play *Threesome*. Set during the Egyptian Revolution, which my friends in Cairo had participated in, I felt passionately that the people I knew and loved there should see it.

Threesome is funny, but about brutal topics: racism, rape, and colonialism. It's the kind of theatrical experience that makes people uncomfortable. That's the point. In the story, the play's main character has to summon tremendous courage to publish her personal experience in a book. By the end of it, she is onstage, naked and alone with the determination to give a voice to others like her.

One day while we were bringing this play to Egypt, I sat in the warm October air on a rooftop garden a stone's chuck from the pyramids. Sitting there, I opened an email from my dad. He proposed we write the book you are holding.

He told me that the time had come to share our experience in a way that might help others. I laughed at the irony, gritted my teeth because I knew it was true, and cried because the words of my best friend arrived to me from across the ocean fragrant with the love—and courage—that only comrades on an awful and wondrous journey know.

There are plenty more books I would like to write—a drug recovery manual for people in the theater (*From Meth-head to Method: An Actor's Journey*), a collection of sacred sex poems (*Beditations*), and a sassy children's adventure novel (*Gus and Gramma at The Guggenheim*). But I'll never write another book like this. Not because it nearly killed me, but because I could never again approximate the profound joy and satisfaction of creating alongside my greatest teacher, my greatest foe, and my greatest friend. I am blessed beyond measure.

Years ago, when I was ten, eleven, and twelve, my favorite thing in the world was to ride with Dad in the mornings to his university, where he would let me sit in the back of his theology classes. Up earlier than usual, early enough to see the sunrise light up the sky in the colors of a Nez Perce blanket, nothing was as thrilling as getting ready— with the self-assured elegance only a prepubescent theologian has—to solve the problems Dad's students found so complicated.

"Two questions, Drew," Dad would say. "You can raise your hand *two times,* no more. Please think carefully, and formulate what you're going to ask before you ask it."

"Okay, Dad! Can I talk about . . . ummm . . . "

"Drew, Drew, Drew. Don't think of what you're going to talk about. Come ready to *listen.* The questions will reveal themselves if you're quiet."

"Okay, Dad! Hey Dad?"

"Yeah."

"I love you. I'm glad you're my dad."

"I love you too, Drew. I'm so glad you're my son."

ACKNOWLEDGMENTS

BRAD

I want to thank my colleagues and students at Multnomah University, a conservative evangelical institution, who have enthusiastically supported me in this project, and many of whom have loved my son Drew since he was a little guy.

Thanks to Gramma Patti, who provided us two great places to write over this past year, both with balconies from which we could hear the ocean's roar and witness its power, giving us many welcome respites from the pressure of writing.

Thanks to Eric and his late husband Eugene, two beautiful men who loved each other for over sixty years and allowed me to see what it looked like for two people to care for each other for so long.

Thanks to Blair Jacobson and to Paul Pastor for their careful and patient editing and for helping us shape our story into something that could be told in less than 500 pages! Words simply cannot express our appreciation for Don Jacobson and the team at Zeal Books. When Don, serving as our agent, presented our book project to several major Christian publishing houses, the response from each of them was, "This is a great book, but we can't publish it." Don felt this book was too important, so he decided to start a new publishing company and make this book his first offering. Then his team of experienced professionals adopted our project as if it were their own. We could not have done this without you guys!

DREW

To Julie and Randy, Jackie and Steve, Dick and Jeanette, Tom and AJ, and all you beautiful Church People who never stopped coming in to hug me even when I tried to claw your eyes out.

To Gramma Patti and Stephen Winter. You are the most magical Fairy Godmother and Fairy Godfather a boy could wish for, and you have sprinkled so much pixie dust on the man this Peter Pan is growing up to be.

To ABLS and Yung Mima. You spent years patiently teaching me what a privileged brat I was, then showed me how to Turn Up against oppression.

To Jessie, my beautiful evangelical dyke sister-shaman. You show me Christ and gave our book its name.

To Abi and Tom at GAYLETTER, and to Julianne, my beautiful Editrix at Mic. You told me I was already a real writer.

To Phillip, Drew, Justin, Nico, and all the kids from Gay Christian Network and Level Ground. You told me that this book was desperately needed.

To Jiji and Katie and Alana, my No Bullsh*t Cheer Team. You never let me think too much or too little of myself or this project, and you have come to love my crazy evangelical family more than an Arab, a WASP, and a Jew ever thought possible.

To Omar, for all the Shining Shimmering Splendor, and for enjoying, or pretending to enjoy, the prose contained herein.

To my brothers at the Electric House: McGuire, Jordy, John, Alejandro, E-man and Danny; and the trio of Lady Angels in Los Angeles: Corrina Gramma, Aspen Mattis, and Aya Tarek. Your strength and integrity and kindness gave me the power to finish this race.

ACKNOWLEDGMENTS

To the Zeal Books team, for your patience with my diva antics, for laughing at my most inappropriate jokes, and for having the hippest looking office allowed to a Christian publisher.

To Blair Jacobson, for giving this book its roots and for kicking through every unfortunate-but-accurate stereotype about your generation of emergent church hipsters in those honey-camel boots of yours.

And finally, to my brilliant publisher-turned-agent-turned-publisher Don Jacobson, and my editor-Abbott Paul Pastor, for becoming my uncle and my brother, for letting me borrow your vision and hope for this project again and again when I had lost my own, and for censoring me with wisdom while loving me without a drop of censorship.

KICKSTARTER CONTRIBUTORS

The book that you are holding in your hands is a special one—creating it has been a team effort from start to finish. The people who supported and shared *Space at the Table*'s Kickstarter project have been a vital part of that team, and without them, this book wouldn't have been possible.

To each of our 602 backers: Thank you! Thank you for believing in this book as much as we do. You helped make this happen.

We'd also like to give a special word of thanks to the following people who contributed to the success of *Space at the Table* in huge ways:

Scott and Susan Boe
Cheryl Canning
Lee and Donnette Castonguay
Jack and Janet Chalfant
Steve and Cheryl Cozette
Anita and Tom Demlow
Susan Lily Frost
Stan and Gina Gibson
Julie Grove
Jeff Harper
Heather Harris
Matt and Jenna Johnson

Ryan Michael Johnson
Kristin Jordan
Andreas and Kelsey Lunden
Kevin and Shelley McBride
Alex and Kaile Moon
Wilson and Amber Rector
Jay Rosenzweig
Dick and Janis Smith
Johnne Syverson
Doug and Debbie Wiens
Wm. Paul Young

And finally, a huge thank you to Clarke Leland and the team at Cascadiom Media who filmed the beautiful video featured in our Kickstarter campaign.

ABOUT THE AUTHORS

Since 1999, **Brad Harper** has been a professor of theology at Multnomah University and Biblical Seminary in Portland, Oregon. From 1986 to 1999, he served as a pastor and church planter in two evangelical churches in St. Louis, Missouri. Because his son is a member of the gay community, Brad has spent years building bridges and friendships there. He has also listened to the coming out stories of many evangelical college students behind the closed door of his office. Over the last several years, Brad has spoken to churches, conferences, pastors' groups, ministry leaders, and hundreds of college and seminary students on the topic of Christianity and homosexuality. Brad is the father of three adult children and lives in Vancouver, Washington, with his wife, Robin. He holds a BA in biblical studies from Biola University, an MDiv from Talbot Seminary, and a PhD in theology from St. Louis University.

Drew Stafford Harper was born in Missouri and raised in St. Louis and Vancouver, Washington. He was educated at New York University and Evergreen State College. Drew is a journalist and an actor, splitting his time (and his wardrobe and furniture) between Manhattan, Los Angeles, Portland, and Cairo. Although he has played a bestselling author on stage, this is his first book in real life.

COMING SOON...

A new book about forgiveness by Dr. Bruce Wilkinson, best-selling author of *The Prayer of Jabez* and *Secrets of the Vine*.

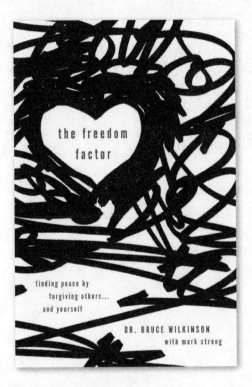

Every pastor we've asked has told us that over 90% of their congregations struggle with forgiveness. What if Jesus really meant it when He said we should forgive someone not just seven times, but seventy times seven? The answer could change your life.

Coming Spring 2016
Visit zealbooks.com/freedom-factor

ZⓔALbooks

Portland, Oregon

Zeal Books is a new publisher dedicated to world-changing ideas. We're focused and founded on love—love for our authors and love for their books. And love makes you zealous. Zeal's commitment to its authors, readers, and accounts is to only publish books we're zealous for—books the world needs.

Visit us online for news, resources, and more, at zealbooks.com, or find us on social media:

 @ZealBks

f facebook.com/zealbks